Uncle Joe, FDR and the Deep State

W. August Mayer

THIS BOOK WOULD NOT HAVE BEEN POSSIBLE WITHOUT THE SUPPORT OF MY LOVELY WIFE PATRICIA, AS WELL AS THE GENEROUS EDITORIAL AND CRITICAL GUIDANCE OF GREGORY POULOS

PRESENTED AS A MONOGRAPH, THE CHAPTERS HAVE BEEN DISPENSED WITH TO PROVIDE THE READER WITH A MORE SEAMLESS EXPERIENCE

UNCLE JOE, FDR AND THE DEEP STATE

W. AUGUST MAYER

SAN FRANCISCO, CA - PIPELINEMEDIA

It really is quite remarkable to be living in times that can still evoke allusions to the finality of the crucible, "standing in the judgment of God's holy fire." Will the distillate be cast of dreck, wrought by a toothless harridan and found unworthy, like Cain's sacrifice, or will it be rendered pure by the all consuming inferno of angelic intercession - once again made fit to ignite the best in man?

Whether this conflagration will cleanse the spirit or destroy it in a malicious act of spite is a story yet to play out, leaving us to ponder; what became of that time - now long past - when all but dullards were consumed by ideas so beautiful?

Unresolved, the question sleeps not; what brought us to this moment, not in the celestial or metaphysical sense, but having navigated to this slice of time where, we trust, our moral center has only been misplaced rather than strangled by the new gods of Baal whose lust for power is boundless?

Listen hard, the pavement throbs, soon may come the cadence of boots, crackling, starched BDUs and that awful snick of bolts going into battery with deadly intent.

Is this not still the home of the brave, granite-like jaw set against the storm or is that now a foolish metaphor past which society has evolved?

A thousand years of light, a thousand years of darkness, history's sinusoidal meter and we at its nexus hoping not to fall back into the vast emptiness that sucks at us with icy breath.

1

Though on our lips now for what might seem like forever - but of late with increasing frequency - come whispers of a concept alien to this society...to the West, the Deep State.

Grasping for understanding, we should avoid the classical social rebel's meme of the "establishment," which though still largely a creature of the left, fails to present the requisite united front as a battering ram. So no, the Deep State isn't just a sub-rosa element of the powers that be. Rather, it's a highly organized, ideologically consistent, revolutionary entity that at the moment is engaged in a soft-coup - for now - an effort to overturn the will of the electorate that spoke loudly on November 8.

An agent in the forced rending of our traditional past, the Deep State can only be seen as the embodiment of an existential threat. In this sense it should be seen as being un-American rather than anti-American; it subverts from within, a traitor, not an invader.

It is massive structurally, consisting of a network of supremely arrogant, highly intelligent and very powerful embedded senior level government employees as well as elite institutions and their leaders who justify their behavior through a process of reasoning that conflates ends and means, creating a "unity of opposites," a term that is entirely consistent with the Marxist dialectic, regardless of whether its practitioners are aware of it by that name or not.

The utopia these people seek to impose on all is the product of cleverly subducting American traditionalism and its driving moral imperatives, Judaism and Christianity.

The core strength [and hence danger] of the Deep State lies in its ability to terraform the information that flows through the nodal gateways that dot the information transmission architecture of the West.

As societal ideological levers, that which gives autocratic elites the ability to present what are assumedly the pertinent and uncontested facts and data-points concerning a matter are the coin of the realm. That they work according to a common playbook relieves the need of the components to coordinate activities across the entire spectrum of the information battle-space. This also has the side and very powerful benefit of decoupling or camouflaging the individuals and organizations that are driving a narrative from any appearance of involvement.

Voila...instant and plausible deniability.

Though the corpus of beliefs, customs, laws, history and the many other elements that come together to form the trademark of a free society represent a massive amount of inertia against revolutionary change, it cannot prevent the glacially slow but nonetheless corrosive effect of a society that has become the classic, "house divided against itself."

Put another way, this means that those who have successfully marched through and weaponized the foundational elements of our republican democracy have gained the ability to continuously reconfigure the American zeitgeist, pushing it ever farther down the pathway that inevitably ends in a dystopian nightmare.

The more that systems involving human interaction gain in complexity, the more useful it is to think about them - analytically - in terms of being living organisms; hence internal warfare mimics the nature of a body beset by an auto-immune disease.

It stands to reason then, to look at threats - to what is now almost literally a body politic - in terms of disease vectors - a primary one of late having its origins in rogue elements that have been ferreted away within the American intelligence colossus.

Though the machinations are complex, the technique is clear, creating a false, but easily digestible, paint by numbers image of a corrupt and even treasonous administration. Thus curated, the news being tossed about can be genuine, elaborately concocted or some mixture thereof.

For example "unmasking" the identities of government officials who, during the natural and responsible exercise of their duties, carry on communications with foreign leaders, provides the Fourth Estate with the grist to spin a damning story.

"News," absent proof, accountability by the author[s] and named sources though highly dubious journalistically, makes a quite effective political weapon - which is of course the intent of those running these operations.

Polemicists are not reporters...

In the current iteration, this is done largely by playing into the running narrative where the public sees "Mr. X" linked with "some Russian," and assumes the worst. News consumers who rely on social-media platforms are especially prone to this type of agitprop or disinformation. Deprived [by choice, and often proudly] of textual content, cognition then becomes a process dominated by repeated exposure to "the pretty colors," about which Marshall McLuhan had an astonishing level of insight.

Freedom and the Deep State are entirely incompatible - matter and anti-matter - which is why if you look closely enough at the process, it's the oligarchs who are now acting through their surrogate army of trained seals - the cultural Marxists - to the crush even minor threats such as freedom of expression on government funded American college campuses which are now, largely "First Amendment free zones," and sometimes even physically hostile environments.

If the Deep State is so threatened by the new marshal in town that it's willing to bring its ruthless game down to the local level, where Make America Great Again baseball caps are considered grounds for justifiable assault, what about the bigger picture?

We are left with the alpha and the omega - Seth Rich and James Hodkinson.

Be mindful that the left does not want to simply prevail in this contest; its idea of justice is nuking an opponent's stadium as a warning to all. In that respect [and actually in numerous other ways] the normative practice of this ideology mimics that of the Muslim jihadists, with whom they maintain a partnership of convenience.

Probably the most public example of this as we go to press is the waddling, Brooklyn born, Arab stealth jihadist Linda Sarsour who went hard-left [Washington's "pussy hat" march] when her Islamist rap ceased getting any attention. In today's media environment, even on the supposedly conservative friendly Fox News, this shrill creature's familial ties to Hamas and her own association with terror linked organizations such as the Islamic Society of North America [ISNA] remain off-limits for discussion.

CASE STUDIES IN SUBVERSIVE DOMESTIC SPY CRAFT
LIARS, HOOKERS AND BEARS

This in compressed format, is one of two real-life examples we will use to illustrate the nature of the kind of operations run by the Deep State as it attempts to remove or politically cripple the president. We believe that it is entirely uncontroversial to characterize the activity as evidence of an attempted soft-coup. This particular case involves - at a minimum - disclosure of classified information [18 U.S. Code § 798], forgery, libel, subornation of perjury, conspiracy, information laundering and prosecutorial abuse at the highest level of American law enforcement - the FBI and its parent, the U.S. Department of Justice - both of which are littered with Obama hold-over, political operatives.

Note that a central player in this affair is Senator John McCain, ostensibly a Republican, but in actuality a gun-for-hire, half-crazed purveyor of influence, whose actions in constantly attacking members of his own party, and his key role in the following operation, strongly point to the Deep State being an equal opportunity employer. The closer one scrutinizes these matters the less difference there is between the Democrat and Republican parties. Of import, McCain has substantial ties with Ukraine. He was awarded by Ukraine President Petro Poroshenko the "Order of Ukraine" and has made numerous visits to the country. The "Affiliated Senior Fellow at the McCain Institute," is David J. Kramer - a leftie out of the Obama administration - who was, "a member of the Ukraine Today media organization's "International Supervisory Council," the enterprise has since folded.

Why is Ukraine important?

Politico, reported in January of 2017, that Ukrainian officials [led by Poroshenko] were secretly working with the Clinton campaign to discredit then candidate Trump. [source, Kenneth P. Vogel and David Stern, *Ukrainian efforts to sabotage Trump backfire*]

The article, a gem-like blockbuster of an expose, prints out to 18 pages.

A few words of caution before we proceed; don't let the comic book-cum tabloid nature of some of the allegations contained in the "dossier" cause you to lose sight of the evil intent that underlies the plot. It remains a deadly serious component in the attempt to convict the President of the United States on false charges, presenting facts not in evidence to create a story consistent with the current plot-line, that Trump is guilty of treason, having forged a quid-pro-quo alliance with Russian strongman Vladimir Putin.

We begin:

Sir Andrew Wood, the former British ambassador to Moscow meets with U.S. Senator John McCain [UK Daily Mail] making him aware of a "dossier" assembled by a former MI6 agent Christopher Steele [sources at MI6 say he never retired] that contained salacious [risibly so] material regarding President Trump. McCain, not terribly familiar with the concept of ethics, manages to get the "dossier" passed along to then FBI director James Comey sometime near the beginning of 2017, compounding the offense by calling it an act of patriotism.

The content of the file was a loosely guarded secret in DC, having been shopped around town for some time to the usual suspects, hard lefties such as David Corn of Mother Jones, the Old Gray Lady herself - the New York Times, American law enforcement and basically anyone who would listen, including BuzzFeed which eventually published it.

Launching the scheme, Steele's company, Orbis Intelligence, was commissioned to prepare the study by an American company, Fusion GPS, a Democrat op-research outfit. At the inception of the undertaking, reports seem to indicate that the initial contract was paid for by the Hillary Clinton presidential campaign [or big-money donors acting on her behalf] but then might have received funding from other sources [see, Grassley, *Letter of Inquiry to Fusion GPS*].

Comey's FBI has admitted to also paying Steele for the "research" meaning that he was likely reimbursed numerous times for the same shoddy work, a neat trick, perhaps one of the reasons why he left his home in the middle of the night and has apparently now gone to ground. So rapid was his departure that lights were left on and his cat was left for safe keeping with a neighbor.

Fusion GPS itself has some intriguing associations.

For example, it had been previously hired by the Russian Bear to lobby against American legislation [the Magnitsky Act, a law providing for sanctions against Russian human rights violations]. By law, Fusion was acting on behalf of a foreign government and was therefore obligated to register under the Foreign Agent Registration Act, but failed to do so according to information developed by Senator Charles Grassley.

Digging deeper...

Most deliciously we have the curious matter of Natalia Veselnitskaya, a non-English speaking Russian attorney [now definitively tied to Russia's FSB - the former KGB -

with a shadowy mission including meeting with Donald Trump Jr., promising she had "anti-Hillary dirt"] whose visa application for entry into the United States had been denied...that was, until the Obama Administration actively became involved - with a supposed nobody - and started pulling some strings.

"Former President Barack Obama's Justice Department allowed Russian attorney Natalia Veselnitskaya to enter the U.S. without a visa, enabling her to lobby President Trump's campaign officials and others in Washington last year. The department cleared the Kremlin-linked lawyer under 'extraordinary circumstances...'" [source, Anna Giaritelli, *Obama allowed Russian lawyer into US under 'extraordinary circumstances'*, Washington Examiner].

Another intriguing aspect of Ms. Veselnitskaya's CV is that she's had a long-standing, working relationship with...Fusion GPS which admits that, "it did work on a lawsuit that involved Veselnitskaya for more than two years...[with her]..." [source, Josh Rogin, *Inside the link between the Russian lawyer who met Donald Trump Jr. and the Trump "dossier"*, Washington Post]

The level of intrigue here is so deep that we will likely never be able to fully plumb its depths, but the stand-out, uncontested facts are that we have a sea of operatives, all positively ID'd as being either directly connected with "Putin's Russia" or having demonstrated extreme animus against President Trump, colluding to chum the waters with the hope of swiftly removing him from office, for among other things...incredibly...working behind the scenes with...the Russians.

Comey was not acting alone, having a major ally, so before we proceed, a brief codicil is necessary to understand the all encompassing nature of the effort to slime President Trump and the original source of the agitprop, the Russians.

CIA Director, John Brennan's [at one time having been an admitted communist as well as allegedly being a closeted Muslim] fingerprints appeared to be visible from the start of this affair. He might have even set the ball rolling before Comey became involved.

According to the UK Guardian:

"...GCHQ's [France's General Directorate for External Security] then head, Robert Hannigan, passed material in summer 2016 to the CIA chief, John Brennan...[it was]...deemed so sensitive it was handled at 'director level'...In late August and September Brennan gave a series of classified briefings to the Gang of Eight [Congress' top leadership]...He told them the agency had evidence the Kremlin might be trying to help Trump to win the presidency...Brennan did not reveal sources but made reference to the fact that America's intelligence allies had provided information. Trump subsequently learned of GCHQ's role...[the source claimed that]...FBI's director, James Comey, altered his position after the election and Trump's victory, becoming "more affirmative" and with a "higher level of concern." [source, *British spies were first to spot Trump team's links with Russia*, Guardian UK]

Despite the machinations of America's top spooks, the "dossier" was so absurd that it didn't pass the smell test - to anyone with a seasoned nose - and few treated it seriously, except of course those whose intent was to use it as an instrument of attempted political assassination. Within the 35 page document, rife with grammatical and spelling errors, is a section alleging that Donald Trump at some point in time had paid Russian hookers to urinate on a bed that had been slept in by President Obama and his wife. If you find that assertion believable [the entire file is available online] then you can stop reading right now.

Attesting to the origin of the document, we turn to someone who should know, Professor Paul Roderick Gregory, a long-time observer and expert on Russian political and business affairs and a Hoover Institution fellow.

In a January 13, 2017 piece in Forbes, *The Trump Dossier Is Fake - And Here Are The Reasons Why*, he wrote:

"As someone who has worked for more than a decade with the microfilm collection of Soviet documents in the Hoover Institution Archives, I can say that the dossier itself was compiled by a Russian, whose command of English is far from perfect and who follows the KGB (now FSB) practice of writing intelligence reports," Gregory continued. "The anonymous author claims to have "trusted compatriots" who knew the roles that each Kremlin insider, including Putin himself, played in the Trump election saga and were prepared to tell him."

But though this crazy quilt of cut-and-paste allegations was privately being laughed about in many corners, Comey ["the DC Boy Scout"] was far from done. He used the FBI's paid for, discredited hit-piece to obtain a FISA court warrant to surveil someone at the barest fringe of the Trump campaign, Carter Page, about whom no action has been initiated, nor is any expected.

Yet the drumbeat continues…

AND THE CRADLE WILL ROCK - COMEY'S ALTITUDE SICKNESS

Over the previous year, through the Summer of 2016 and up through the Fall election, FBI Director James Comey had begun a pattern of acting far outside his statutory authority in numerous matters, most publicly, regarding the non-investigation of the Hillary Clinton email scandal.

On July 5, 2016, just a few weeks after having made the announcement that his agency was re-opening the investigation [in itself highly irregular as it is official DOJ policy not to comment on such matters] Comey called a press conference during which he proffered a series of "offenses/irregularities" that seemed to foretell charging documents indicting the Democrat nominee. During this performance, the Director's body language - hinting at a blockbuster announcement - was worthy of a Shakespearean actor.

At the end of his presentation, though, instead of referring the matter to the AG for final disposition he, to the surprise of many who were watching the eerie event live, recommended against charging her, stating that the apparent offenses lacked "intent."

Informed members of the public, not to mention legal commentators, of all political stripes, were left slack-jawed since the supposedly exonerating "lack of intent" relied upon a non-existent legal standard, especially in cases where there was a pattern of intentional and reckless disregard for the handling of state secrets, in Hillary's case including information pertaining to America's most highly secured intelligence operations, Special Access Programs [SAPS].

The upshot of this was that "Lurch" Comey publicly elbowed the AG aside, despite the fact that Lynch, as head of the DOJ [and the rather significant fact that she was Comey's boss] was the only party who had the constitutional authority make such a determination.

Comey's erratic behavior engendered such a sense of crisis among the FBI's directorate that on May 9, 2017, Deputy Assistant Director of FBI Rod J. Rosenstein felt moved to draft an extraordinarily critical document castigating the then Director's behavior to such a degree that it amounted to a recommendation to dismiss him:

"Almost everyone agrees that the Director made serious mistakes; it is one of the few issues that unite people of diverse perspectives. The director was wrong to usurp the Attorney General's authority on July 5, 2016, and announce his conclusion that the case should be closed without prosecution...It is not the function of the Director to make such an announcement...The

Director now defends his decision by asserting that he believed attorney General Loretta Lynch had a conflict. But the FBI Director is never empowered to supplant federal prosecutors and assume command of the...Department...Although the President has the power to remove an FBI director, the decision should not be taken lightly...[pregnant pause]...I agree with the nearly unanimous opinions of former Department officials. The way the Director handled the conclusion of the email investigation was wrong. As a result, the FBI is unlikely to regain public and congressional trust until it has a Director who understands the gravity of the mistakes and pledges never to repeat them. Having refused to admit his errors, the Director cannot be expected to implement the necessary corrective actions." [emphasis added, source, Candice Norwood and Elaine Godfrey, *Rosenstein's Case Against Comey, The Atlantic*]

On that same day, Comey was fired by the President.

But the intrigue had just begun; the now ex-Director would exact his revenge. Whether it was a contingency for this eventuality or had long been planned, given the way the cards were played, it certainly appears to be the latter.

Previous to his firing, President Trump and Comey had a private meeting during which many topics were covered, including mention of the investigation of Trump's former national security advisor, Lt. Gen Michael Flynn.

Sometime subsequent to the meeting, the FBI Director then assembled what he now represents as "contemporaneous notes" [doing so on a government computer] regarding what had allegedly transpired during the meeting. Such conversations and any documents containing transcripts or 'contemporaneous notes" clearly fall under the definition of Executive Privilege, meaning that they are undoubtedly protected governmental communication, the leaking of which is a felony.

Nonetheless within these "notes" Comey alleged that the President had attempted to obstruct the Flynn investigation, although both men agree that the President only asked if it would be possible to give Flynn a bit of a break since the matter seemed minor, an accusation that Flynn had lobbied on behalf of Turkey in the past.

In an astounding public admission of criminal action, Comey stated in Congressional testimony that he gave a copy of the documents to his "close friend," Daniel C. Richman, the Paul J. Kellner, Professor of Law at Columbia Law School and a former federal prosecutor, upon the agreement that Richman would then hand them off to the New York Times, a "dead drop" lifted from a bad movie script.

"I asked a friend of mine to share the content of the memo with a reporter," Comey told Collins. "I didn't do it myself for a variety of reasons, but I asked him to, because I thought that might prompt the appointment of a special counsel."

According to plan, this is exactly what transpired and thus the President of the United States now faces a "Special Counsel/Inquisition/fishing trip" headed by ex-FBI Director Robert Mueller, who has hired a number of highly biased Democrat prosecutors one of whom, Jeannine Rhee, actually represented the Clinton Foundation in a racketeering case.

Despite the fact that these stories read like LSD laced parodies of a John le Carré novel and that all of the above players either can be connected to Russia or have contracted "Trump Derangement Syndrome," it remains the Deep State's drum-beat that Donald J. Trump, with the help of Russian operatives, hacked the election and now continues to act as an agent of influence answering to Vlad Putin.

These vignettes should provide the reader with a sense of how the Deep State operates, not only entirely above the law but in this and numerous other cases, actually in collusion with U.S. intelligence agencies, federal "law enforcement," and unsurprisingly, their trusty scribes at the WashPost/NYT and among cable television's self-righteous talking suits.

WARNING: STEEP LEARNING CURVE AHEAD

Perhaps now is the appropriate time to make the observation that none of what follows will ever make sense; the jumble of events, names, places, charges, counter-charges and intrigue will forever remain impenetrable unless citizens of a serious bent open themselves to unlearning, or at least massively re-evaluating a lot of what has been taken for Gospel in American history, for nearly the last 100 years.

For many, the biggest hurdle that must be overcome - and it's huge - can also serve as a lens through which we might be better situated to understand and provide a frame of reference for the threat we see coming out of DC and the I95 corridor.

As is sometimes the case in such matters, starting with a bit of a historical review is often the only way we can work towards understanding what is happening today and why it is taking place.

The first lesson - the red pill - will be the one most difficult for many to accept, since it deals with how almost everyone [that is the dwindling numbers who are still aware of the event] perceive the Second World War and the events surrounding it. To this group of people, WWII was the "good war," the conflict that saved Western Civilization and eventually brought down what Ronald Reagan correctly labeled the "Evil Empire."

We feel compelled by the evidence to challenge that conclusion to the point of suggesting, as have a relatively few brave revisionist historians and writers examining the era, that though the United States and its allies won the conflict, the ultimate outcome of the war remains very much in doubt.

Reducing the idea to its essentials, the theory we will advance is that on VJ Day, though Hitler and the Nazis had been crushed and Imperial Japan incinerated, a far more malevolent presence, the Soviet Union, would go on to subjugate Eastern Europe for the next half-century and domestically [and more insidiously, in perhaps a preponderance of the cases] was actually paid to penetrate the government of the United States, actively working with domestic fifth columnists to extend the grasp of what remains the globe's most threatening ideology, Marxism-Leninism.

In establishing the outermost structure of the covalent components of the Deep State, and mindful of what David Horowitz has termed the "Unholy Alliance" between the Marxists and the jihadists; though the sons of the god who hates continue to ply their nasty trade, they do so under cover provided by the left. Deprived of the protection and influence bestowed by the Open Society Foundation types of the world, it is this author's considered opinion that the jihadist threat in the West could be rolled up in a relatively short time…the process would not be pretty, but then our side didn't throw the first punch.

The documentary evidence underlying this contrarian reading of history is rich in primary sourced material, for example, John Haynes & Harvey Klehr - *Venona: Decoding Soviet Espionage in America*, Jerrold & Leona Schecter - *Sacred Secrets: How Soviet Intelligence Operations Changed American History*, M. Stanton Evans & Herbert Romerstein - *Stalin's Secret Agents - The Subversion of Roosevelt's Government*, and most recently the extraordinarily well-written compendium of related information, *American Betrayal: The Secret Assault on our Nation's Character*, by Diana West.

The case that these researchers make is compelling. Distressingly, the deeper you probe, the more solid the evidence appears.

Part of the reason we can make such a positive assertion is because it's backed up by hard data, as in 1943 an arm of American intelligence, actually the precursor of the NSA [an agency that had its beginnings 100 years ago, when Herbert Yardley was designated to head the Cipher Bureau of Military Intelligence, that eventually morphed into NSA proper in 1952] succeeded in partially cracking the coding system that the Soviets were using to manage the huge number of spies and fellow travelers that Stalin had infiltrated into the country during Franklin Roosevelt's four successive administrations.

The job that the early code breakers had undertaken became known as the Venona Project. It was very highly classified and few knew about its existence. A long-term project, it was finally canceled in 1980.

The suggestion here is that the information that had been obtained by decoding - though it represented only a small part of the whole - was so politically explosive that it took an act of Congress to even partially declassify and release some of the transcripts in 1995.

This might help explain why to this day FDR remains a leftist demi-god; bottled up for nearly 80 years, even the most damning truths lose much of what might have been their impact, if the information had been released somewhat more contemporaneously.

There was a very good reason for the hesitancy by the Feds to open the files, because when looked at as a whole, combined with classified state secrets that the Russians made available for a short period of time post the fall of the Soviet Union [Boris Yeltsin opened Soviet archival material from the KGB, the Soviet Central Committee and the presidential archives in 1991, but that glimpse into the blackest of black holes was quickly slammed shut when Russia returned to it totalitarian comfort zone] it's impossible not to conclude that starting in the early part of the 20th century, the Soviet Union deployed the most sophisticated attack ever launched against the United States.

The operation was so cunningly planned and executed that the dictator was able to seed a thousand spies [quite possibly many times that] into the country, a daunting number for sure but one whose effectiveness was substantially magnified by the internal subversion that was carried on by untold thousands of American citizens who were either outright members of the Communist Party USA [CPUSA] or Soviet sympathizers.

Though the process got its start near the end of the 1920's it gained additional traction as the economic hard times continued into the next decade. But it was not until Europe went to war that the program became a top Soviet priority.

In what is now considered, by some to be a rather mild judgment we learn that:

"Based on what we know today, it appears that hundreds of such people - perhaps thousands - got hired by the government in the early to mid 1940s, reinforcing the already numerous corps of agents named by [Whittaker] Chambers in the prewar era..." [source, M. Stanton Evans & Herbert Romerstein, *Stalin's Secret Agents*, Threshold Editions, 2012, pg. 99]

So great was the level of influence that by the mid 1940s, J. Edgar Hoover's FBI was cranking out what should have been heart-attack inducing reports:

"It has become increasingly clear in the investigation of this case that there are a tremendous number of persons employed in the United States government who are Communists and who strive daily to advance the cause of Communism and destroy the foundations of this government...Today nearly every department or agency of this government is infiltrated with them in varying degree. To aggravate the situation, they appear to have concentrated most heavily in those departments which make policy, particularly in the international field, or carry it into effect . . . [including] such organizations as the State and Treasury departments, FEA, OSS, WPB, etc." [source, ibid, *1946 Memo from Special Agent Guy Hottel to FBI Director Hoover*, pg. 99]

Also from the files of America's domestic security agency, which remarkably are still available on the FBI website:

"Many young leftists in the early 1930s had entered the government in the early throes of the New Deal and embraced a Communist siren under whose call significant numbers of them were willing to pass along valuable information to the Soviet Union during the war. A general leftist tilt in the government meant that these ideologues blended well into the Washington bureaucracy while keeping their strong Soviet sympathies largely hidden. The tradecraft of Soviet intelligence personnel, the well honed Communist Party tradition of conspiracy, and a lack of concern in the Roosevelt administration towards Soviet spying meant that little of this growing Soviet intelligence web was found except by accident in the opening years of the war." [source, John F. Fox Jr. FBI Historian, FBI *Counterintelligence Before Venona*]

In an effort to set the table as it were it must be remembered that at the turn of the Twentieth Century - "more innocent" times - declaring oneself a communist was surprisingly uncontroversial despite the troubling fact that during this period of time the CPUSA [which was part of the Comintern, the Soviet's global subversion operation] was run directly out of the Kremlin and this was not a particularly well guarded relationship.

Traveling back some 170 years to the point of origin - the *Manifesto of the Communist Party* - that was written by Marx and Engels in December, 1847 and published in February, 1848, as a general proposition, communism became popular for two reasons, first the ideology is compelling:

Theories that promise an Eden-like existence for little in exchange will always have a natural constituency. When seen in its totality, Marxism is at its most base level a conspiracy theory. It makes it sound reasonable for citizens to believe that it's possible to sidestep poor life choices and naturally occurring disastrous events by taking confiscatory action against the "small number of greedy capitalists," the ones who are supposedly responsible for one's economic fate. That this was a period in which much of the world was mired in a depression that caused catastrophic social dislocation, certainly fed into that belief.

The second reason being that the public was - by necessity - kept ignorant of what was really going on in the Soviet "paradise" and unless/until citizens become aware of real world examples of the death and destruction that Marxism inevitably brings, it's difficult to argue the contra position since the utopian promise is so seductive.

This basic appeal should not be allowed to cloud the tremendous skill, not to mention audacity that the Soviets displayed in the manifest ways they were able to conceal to the outside world, their system's horrendous crimes so pervasive that, because Stalin wanted it that way, people were starving to death, literally dropping dead on the streets in Russia's major cities.

That in America's time of greatest vulnerability, the effort had a kindred spirit of sorts who occupied the highest office in the nation certainly served to cloak the ideology's inherent evil and hasten its acceptance.

Why this was so is still hard to fathom. It grates against the storybook - man on a great white horse - mental image that American citizens had always been led to believe about their presidents.

Roosevelt telegraphed his odd affection for the Russian communists alarmingly early in his first term, when on November 16, 1933 - breaking with the precedent established by the four previous occupants of the White House: Wilson, Harding, Coolidge and Hoover, of refusing to recognize the Bolsheviks - he, with the stroke of a pen did just that.

In response to such immediate and unexpected good fortune, Maxim Litvinov, the Soviet Commissar of Foreign Affairs handed the "leader of the free world," a letter filled with the kind of duplicitous promises the Soviets were already noted for making…and breaking, in which he, according to an account by the long-time Chicago Tribune journalist, Chesly Manly reporting - in what can only be called a spirit of disbelief:

"…solemnly pledged his government "to refrain from interfering in any manner in the internal affairs of the United States" and to restrain all persons and organizations under Moscow's control "from any act overt or overt liable in any way whatsoever to injure the tranquility, prosperity, order or security" of the United States…only a few minutes after leaving the White House [Litvinov met with other Russian official in the Soviet embassy] vigorously rubbing his hands and gave this gleeful account of the negotiations: 'Well, it's all in the bag. They wanted us to recognize the debts we owed them and I promised we were going to negotiate. But they did not know we were going to negotiate until doomsday. The next one was a corker; they wanted us to promise freedom of religion in the Soviet Union, and I promised that too. I was very much prompted to offer that I would personally collect all the Bibles and ship them over." [Chesly Manly, *The Twenty Year Revolution: From Roosevelt To Eisenhower*, Regnery, 1954, pg. 32-33. Fortunately this wrecking ball of a document is available in its entirety online in .pdf format courtesy of the Ludwig von Mises Institute]

President Roosevelt; fool, fellow traveler or? There is no reassuring answer.

It stands to reason then, that being served up the opportunity to work in such a target rich environment, Soviet intelligence was able to run this alarmingly effective global intelligence/espionage/sabotage/disinformation campaign in the face of almost no opposition.

Aside from sheer denial, internally fabricated disinformation and a phalanx of KGB trained agents posing as journalists pushing the Big Lie as part of a united front to mask the realities inside the Soviet "utopia," the Marxists had collaborators in the Western media who were willing to write copy in a manner pleasing to their long-distance brethren.

Here we are referring to people such as the Pulitzer Prize winning New York Times journo, Walter Duranty who managed to conveniently look the other way and actually defend the bloody Soviet regime while tens of millions were starved to death in Ukraine or were worked or frozen to a similar fate in the Gulags.

The depth of Duranty's deception was only surpassed by the intellectual impact fabricated reportage had upon literate Americans:

"There is no famine or actual starvation nor is there likely to be." - New York Times, Nov. 15, 1931

"Any report of a famine in Russia is today an exaggeration or malignant propaganda." - New York Times, August 23, 1933

"Enemies and foreign critics can say what they please. Weaklings and despondents at home may groan under the burden, but the youth and strength of the Russian people is essentially at one with the Kremlin's program, believes it worthwhile and supports it, however hard be the sledding." - New York Times, December 9, 1932

"You can't make an omelet without breaking eggs." - New York Times, May 14, 1933 [source, Arnold Beichman, *Pulitzer Winning Lies*, The Weekly Standard, 2003]

Duranty was not alone...in another of many examples we have Eugene Lyons, a communist sympathizer who served as the United Press Agency's Moscow representative from 1928-1934. Lyons' journey back from Stalinism was recounted in the two books he wrote on the subject, *The Red Decade* and *Assignment in Utopia* [see, Diana West, *American Betrayal*, St. Martin's Griffin, pg. 95]

However the single most significant factor in making this level of infiltration possible was that upon taking office, FDR via his New Deal, created dozens and dozens of new federal agencies that eventually came to employ millions of people.

As a stand-alone this was a bold move by an already out of control chief executive to push the nation towards socialism. That much of the vast new bureaucratic state would have been found unconstitutional had not FDR threatened the Supreme Court in what infamously became known as the "Court Packing" scandal, was unnervingly Soviet-like in its disregard for democratic norms.

Roosevelt's style, self-confidence and the level of support it garnered from the press was so overwhelming that even taking into account the avalanche of change he had embarked upon, his critics were relatively few, cowed into silence.

However, those who dared defy FDR's, "happy days are here again" feel-goodism, had little reason to hold much back.

Concluded the aforementioned Manly, referencing a key component of FDR's explosive governmental expansion, the Office of War Information [OWI], which was:

"...loaded with draft dodgers, red revolutionists, and a scum of European refugees who pretended to sell America to the world but made it their business to sell Communist Russia to America." [West, pg.115]

Though it remains a truism that wars invariably degrade civil liberties while strengthening the power of the central state, the magnitude of Roosevelt's expansion of the federal government's reach - well before the commencement of the Second World War - remains breathtaking.

In 1933 the federal government employed a bit less than 500,000 people, but by 1945 the figure [not including the military] was 3.5 million, an over 700% increase, and many of these agencies had extraordinary [read dictatorial] powers.

Already having been referred to acerbically, let's examine this agency in greater detail since it was the duty of the OWI to actively manage what the American people were expected to think about the war. It did this by manipulating and creating a benign looking smokescreen via newspapers, radio broadcasts and other forms of media to model a nominally pro-American narrative that was both Soviet friendly and supportive of Roosevelt's extreme progressivism, heretofore an alien concept in the United States.

"During World War II, Franklin Roosevelt purposely avoided taking the same path as Woodrow Wilson when he considered the need to mobilize public opinion. Roosevelt's Office of War Information [OWI]...hired thousands of writers, artists and advertisers to sell war..." [source, Nancy Gentile Ford, *Issues Of War And Peace*, Greenwood Press, 1954, pg. 187]

In a glimpse of what was to come, from the beginning of his administration it became clear that FDR was keenly interested in social engineering. We know this because the OWI had a predecessor, the Federal Art Project [FAP] which fell under the jurisdiction of the Works Progress Administration [WPA], the largest arm of Roosevelt's expanded bureaucracy.

In many cases, "expansion" isn't a strong enough term as the FAP alone employed "tens of thousands of artists," who churned out an untold number of commissioned "murals, easel paintings, sculpture, graphic art, posters, photography, theatre scenic design, and arts and crafts." [see, Wiki]

It wasn't coincidental that the motif invoked throughout FDR's patriotic media campaign eerily mirrored Lenin and then Stalin's "revolutionary" art. Ignoring the pictorial content and Cyrillic script, the feeling and vibe were identical.

"The influence of the amateur theater movement on professional drama in the United States cannot be stressed enough. It made "hundreds of thousands of workers theater-conscious," and by linking up labor organizations with the theater, it laid the basis for the subscription system that supported the work of professional leftist theaters such as the Theater Union...Just like in Soviet Russia and the Weimar Republic, the work of these amateur and semi-professional theater groups was often marked by the overt theatricality of agitprop." [source, Ilka Saal, *New Deal Theater: The Vernacular Tradition in American Political Theater,* Pallgrave-McMillan, 2007, pg. 57]

One of the primary reasons why the Soviets devoted so much time and energy to influence the public by co-opting the arts was because Marxist theory had a novel way of outflanking the growing military prowess of the Nazis about whom they were quite worried as well as the democratic governments of the West which constituted a threat by their very existence.

The Soviets were greatly alarmed when the Nazis came to power in 1933, seeing the wedding of Germany's vast industrial might and scientific expertise with an interventionist ideology [National State Socialism] similar to their own. This was viewed as a genuine threat to their plan for world domination through revolutionary communism.

They were also enraged that their street-fighters had just been left black-and-blue [if they were lucky] by Hitler's brown shirts who man-handled them in the streets of Germany's largest cities

Stalin and his advisors in analyzing how to preemptively deal with the increasingly likely possibility of warfare, saw in the potential conflict elements that might be manipulable via the Marxist-Leninist doctrine of engaging the enemy in a war of ideas, which could be fashioned to denigrate the Nazis politically, ideologically and culturally.

The first real example of this took the form of a harsh critique by the Comintern of fascism, calling it "bourgeoisie socialism" - intimating that it was simplistic and unscientific compared to the complexities involved in the Marxist dialectic. Thus the Reds constructed a veneer of intellectual superiority to disguise what was really just a blood-feud between two brutal thugs. Efforts to repurpose language, including redefining words themselves [witness marriage between a man and woman, transformed into marriage, an ill-defined and open ended legal relationship between at least two people, casting aside traditional gender considerations] complemented the larger program designed to destabilize institutions through infiltration and the creation of front organizations controlled by Moscow. Nowhere was this aspect of the conflict more visible than in the infiltration of the Western press and popular literature by writers with a collectivist point of view, either party members or, ideological but non-attached supporters...fellow travelers.

As heretofore referenced, by the early 1930s, though the Reds already had established substantial beachheads within the federal bureaucracy they had more ambitious targets in mind, Hollywood to be exact.

In the United States, frequent movie going was the norm not the exception, with well *over 60% of the public frequenting their local theaters at least once a week.* Though radio was an up and coming communication technology, it just couldn't match the impact of big budgets, good stories, [often] superb acting and lavishly choreographed imagery. When "the technique" was then mated with "heroes" and "heroines" created by Hollywood's rigidly controlled star system you had an historical, demi-version of the Internet, a kind of cultural underlayment which helped define the times.

The impetus behind the Soviet's efforts to organize writers into a revolutionary entity was the *Soviet Writers' Congress 1934: The Debate on Socialist Realism and Modernism* where it was proclaimed that, "literature is a social weapon, that it expresses the struggle between the classes," and a little more poetically:

> *"One cannot be an engineer of human souls without knowing the technique of literary work,* and it must be noted that the technique of the writer's work possesses a large number of specific peculiarities." [section 5, *Fascism and Literature*]

As the communist archival resource, Marxists.org, explains the significance of the event:

> "The Soviet Writers Congress was held in August 1934, five years into the ultra-left "Third Period" of the Comintern, shortly afterwards abandoned in favour of the "Popular Front" policy. The thrust of the Comintern's cultural policy at this time, was to gather around the Comintern leading writers and intellectuals in all countries on the basis of a very sharp anti-fascist line, in which its opponents were frequently labeled as 'social-fascists.'"

Though FDR's "thousands" of artists and writers had the ability to work the party line into their creations, their power to influence the public was far less than that of the established big name authors and screenplay writers,

Hemmingway, Dashiell Hammett, Howard Koch, Ring Lardner and Dalton Trumbo for example, who joined various affinity groups directed by Moscow, were then introduced to the Soviet Marxist version of the AP Stylebook.

"The earnestness that these true believers displayed remains impressive, and the effort remains the most successful political organization of big-time American writers ever. *"The League of American Writers* [presided over by Donald Ogden Stewart] was established by the *First American Writers Congress - April 26-28, 1935. It was allied with the International Union of Revolutionary Writers* [IURW] as well as the *International Association of Writers for the Defense of Culture* and was the American equivalent of the *British League of Writers*. A year later in 1936 The Hollywood Anti-Nazi League was formed." [*League of American Writers*, Wiki]

After the fact, Congress half-heartedly investigated the communist influence in Hollywood, until the effort fell victim to a goose-stepping media that stubbornly, in the face of such evidence, refused to acknowledge its own collusion with the Reds during the war and succeeded in passing off the various attempts to expose what was a genuine threat by the United States' most hostile foreign power, sarcastically as "red baiting" by "reactionaries" and followers of Senator Joseph McCarthy:

"Mr. Tavenner: Will you give us the names of those who were in attendance at the meeting, who were members of the Communist Party?"

Mr. Berkeley: "...also at the meeting was Donald Ogden Stewart, Dorothy Parker was a writer...her husband Allen Campbell...my old friend Dashiell Hammett, who is now in jail in New York for his activities..." [source, United States Congress, *House Committee On Un-American Activities Hearings*, 1951-1952, Volume II pg. 1586]

In a race that wasn't even close, the film, "Mission to Moscow" was the hands-down winner as the most over-the-top, major Hollywood pro-Marxist propaganda effort of the period.

It was all but commissioned by FDR [screen play written by the aforementioned communist Howard Koch] who prevailed upon Joseph E. Davies an American lawyer who had served as Ambassador to Moscow [1936-1938], to become involved in the project, turning his best-selling book into a movie. Released in 1943, it was subsequently seen by millions of Americans.

Though a bit stiff and heavy-handed by today's standards, the movie begins in a period correct manner, with an avuncular, sharply dressed and seated Joseph Davies - drafted to play himself in order to lend the movie with an air of authenticity and gravitas.

After a brief setup he then launches into a pro-Soviet soliloquy bemoaning the unkind way Stalin and the USSR were being treated by Western leaders.

"When I was your ambassador in Russia, I little expected to write "Mission to Moscow," much less to see it projected on screen. But when Germany attacked Russia, the Soviet Union became one of the nations fighting Hitler. And it was a desperate hour. If Hitler were to destroy the Red armies and to smash the Soviet Union, the three aggressor nations would dominate Europe, Asia, and Africa. The riches of these three continents and the enslaved labor of 3/4ths of the population of the world would be harnessed to conquer the rest of the earth. The Americas would be next. U.S. unity among the forces fighting Hitler was vital. Nothing, as I saw it, was more important than that the fighting nations should understand and trust each other. There was so much prejudice and misunderstanding of the Soviet Union..."

That established, Davies then delivers his judgment of Soviet intentions:

"But while in Russia, I came to have a very high respect for the integrity and the honesty of the Soviet leaders. I respected the honesty of their convictions, and they respected mine. I also came back with a firm conviction that these people were sincerely devoted to world peace, and that they and their leaders only wanted to live in a decent world as good neighbors in a world at peace."

The movie was of course reviewed by an eager New York Times, actually its long time film-critic Bosley Crowther, who later went on to attack "McCarthyism" and "the isolationists" in Congress a not too deft reference to the Republican minority.

It doesn't take Crowther very long to drop into a pro-Soviet polemic, at one point siding with Stalin's show trial purge of the USSR's old guard [1936-1938 - the very period of time during which Davies was assigned as ambassador] alleging they were part of a plot led by Trotsky, the Nazis and "the Japs" to seize power from the assumedly saintly Stalin.

As he writes:

"With boldness unique in film ventures, which usually evade all issues, it comes out sharply and frankly for an understanding of Russia's point of view. It says with a confident finality that Russia's leaders saw, when the leaders of other nations dawdled, that the Nazis were a menace to the world. And it has no hesitancy whatever in stepping on a few tender toes...Particularly will it anger the so-called Trotskyites with its visual re-enactment of the famous "Moscow trials." For it puts into the record for millions of moviegoers to grasp an admission that the many "purged" generals and other leaders were conspirators in a plot engineered by Trotsky with the Nazis and the Japs to drain the strength of Russia and make it an easy victim for conquest."

The review lags on until midpoint where Crowther, who was on the Times' payroll for 40 years and was supposedly quite intellectually gifted, then makes a whopper of a claim, that unnamed "reactionaries" started the war and that Stalin was actually a victim!

"In short, it says quite clearly that reactionaries permitted the war and that Russia, far from earlier suspicion, is a true and most reliable ally." [source, Bosley Crowther, *Review: Mission to Moscow*, New York Times, 1943]

Aside from the fact that this characterization elevated the blood soaked Stalin above America's hereditary ally Britain, it conveniently ignored the fact that Hitler had an accomplice in starting World War II, his name...Josef Stalin.

But despite the great success of Roosevelt's "public opinion modeling," the natives who made it possible, the artists, were becoming restless. As the OWI and allied programs continued to unfold and expand they fell under increasing criticism; from the outside by Republican Congressmen and from within, mostly by disgruntled writers and artists whose sensibilities were offended by being so closely directed and controlled. The most common complaint about the OWI was that FDR saw it as a dual use weapon. In addition to its primary charge of stoking the "right kind" of patriotism, it became impossible to separate it from his political campaign apparatus.

One can only imagine the instant outrage that would immediately accompany a modern president establishing such a huge bureaucracy, paid for with tax dollars in order to keep his image burnished and used as a tool against his political opponents.

As was typically the case in the FDR administration, the "alphabet soup" agencies were huge and inefficient - though even by these standards the OWI was massive. But then so was its mission, as OWI's policies affected nearly everything having to do with the dissemination of information, both in the U.S. as well as in foreign outposts.

Consider its array of bureaus and branches:

"Management Branch, Domestic Branch, Book and Magazine Bureau, Foreign News Bureau, Graphics Bureau, Motion Picture Bureau, News Bureau, Radio Bureau, Special Services, Overseas Branch, Overseas Intelligence, Communication Control, Communication Facilities, News and Features, Outpost Service Bureau, Overseas Motion Pictures, Overseas Publications, Radio Program Bureau, New York Regional Office and the San Francisco Regional Office." [source, *U.S. Government Printing Office*]

It was through this kind of amoebic expansion that the federal budget exploded from $8.9 billion in 1939 to over $95 billion in 1945, a ten-fold increase in a mere 6 years.

No longer a secret, but unbeknownst to the public [and still largely unacknowledged] the OWI had been deeply penetrated by Stalin's agents and fellow travelers, for example Owen Latimore, the Deputy Director of the OWI, Pacific was identified by the Senate Internal Security Subcommittee as a Soviet agent. But then so were Philip Keeney, Irving Lerner, Peter Rhodes, Christina Krotkova and Flora Wovschin, all of whom were at one time employed by the OWI.

There was little in society that remained unaffected by this level of change:

"Scores of newspapers were denied the privilege of the mails under the authority of the 1917 Espionage Act, which remained in effect. The Office of Censorship restricted the content of press reports and radio broadcasts and censored personal mail entering or leaving the country. The Office of War Information put the government's spin on what-ever it deigned to tell the public, and the military authorities censored news from the battlefields, sometimes for merely political reasons. The government seized more than 60 industrial facilities - sometimes entire industries, for example, railroads, bituminous coal mines, meatpacking firms - most of them in order to impose employment conditions favorable to labor unions engaged in disputes with the management." [source, *Foundation For Economic Education*]

Interception of personal communication, censorship, working hand-in-glove with leftist unions, flooding the American consciousness via the media with a steady stream of ideologically approved propaganda...

Sound familiar?

The subtext of the storyline was designed with a more sinister domestic purpose in mind. Roosevelt was inculcating the average citizen into the new reality, to feel warm and fuzzy about the burgeoning, centrally planned, quasi-collectivist state that was now in the business of redistributing income - a concept central to Marxism.

On a practical level he was acclimating the public to a malignant philosophy of governance, one based upon the cynical equation that citizens required the active guidance by "experts in Washington who know better," and were empowered to, at will intrude into their everyday affairs, as if they were helpless children without the intervention of the bureaucrats. The second postulate of the new geometry was actually more on the order of an a priori assertion; that this monstrous new creation was somehow consistent with America's founding principles.

Thus arose the outline of the soon to be "American nanny" state, though that juxtaposition is certainly a philosophical contradiction. Left unstated, it was clear that he who controlled the burgeoning apparatus of government could greatly influence public perception. Though seeing the Constitution stretched beyond recognition might have induced heart attacks among the Founding Fathers, one can imagine the document's chief author, James Madison's head exploding upon seeing the damage being done to his [our] beloved document in such a short period of time.

As injurious as all of this was to America's ideals of liberty, freedom and limited government, it was nonetheless true that the nation was in far deeper trouble than was realized because of the radically different way that America and the Soviet Union were able to present themselves to the world.

The Soviet Union was a police state; as closed a society as Lenin, Stalin and later strongmen could make it. The only light that leaked out of that black hole was on the order of controlled releases. This made it difficult [a problem for free societies everywhere when confronting totalitarianism] to even establish reasonably accurate baselines for the most mundane information such as literacy rates, mortality statistics, GDP etc., whereas the Soviet's "Great Satan" was an open book.

Such a disparity in the ability to obtain reasonably correct information gave the Soviets an advantage. Though this didn't give it the capacity to assume whatever nature it wanted to project, it could certainly round the edges off its horrific reality.

No ventriloquist, America was what it was.

The fact is that Marxism is an ideology of permanent, never ending warfare and the Soviets were extraordinarily adroit and successful in exporting its brand of revolutionary ardor across Europe and the United States.

But, and this is critically important, the nature, audacity and sheer scope of Stalin's operation was totally unlike anything coming out of the West.

Understandably, the United States had developed a more than moderate level of expertise in the typical elements of spy craft, cracking codes, rudimentary electronic and of course personal surveillance, disinformation campaigns and other intrigues.

But the Soviets under Stalin used their intelligence capability in both a passive as well as active sense, establishing hundreds of spy-cells containing thousands of operatives across the nation, many of whom were actually employed by Uncle Sam - deep-cover operatives seeded throughout the highest levels of the federal bureaucracy.

In organizing these Red Cells, the Soviets wrote the book, with the network usually comprised of small groups, perhaps five individuals living fairly close to each other who got together perhaps a couple of times a week to discuss and absorb the ever changing party-line. Operating independently with so many degrees of separation meant that even if discovered, the damage would be minimal due to the compartmental nature of the structure allowing for the overall network to remain intact.

In that regard, as scholar and mathematician Nassim Nicholas Taleb might argue, this type of structure was - contrasted against the open American system - far more "anti-fragile," because it was organizationally strongly self-indemnified against unexpected, outliers, in Taleb's parlance, "Black Swan" or highly improbable events that though rare are catastrophic in effect.

So while the West could successfully in specific instances obtain transmissions, diplomatic messages and other types of classical intelligence, it was far beyond our capacity or even our thought process to be able to deploy the type of counter-network required to - in a direct, hands on manner actually create and - during critical periods - control Soviet policy.

In the United States though decisions of great import were being made by key Soviet operatives: Alger Hiss [Assistant Secretary of State] Lauchlin Currie [economic advisor to Roosevelt] Harry Dexter White [Treasury Department who worked closely with Treasury's Secretary Morgenthau, himself rather soft on interpreting the Soviet threat] Julius

Robert Oppenheimer [chief physicist and Director of the Manhattan Project] and the Soviet's biggest trophy, Harry Hopkins, FDR's right hand man, an appellation probably minimizing his importance because throughout much of the war he actually lived in the White House, in the Lincoln "bedroom" to be specific. Hopkins was later identified as, *Soviet Agent 19.*

Morgenthau in devising his post-war plan for Europe was greatly influenced by the traitor White whose vengeful notion of reducing Germany to a preindustrial society through a policy of salt-the-earth "unconditional surrender" was plucked directly off the lips of Stalin. It also, as Evans and Romerstein noted, "infuriated" the U.S. military high command [notably General Marshall] who knew that it would drive the proud Germans into a nation of dead-enders who would fight to the last man, thus prolonging the war to the detriment of the United States while "Uncle Joe" could sit back and watch his treachery play out.

To gain as full a sense as possible of the level to which FDR's war fighting capability had been compromised by Soviet infiltration, the following is a more extensive listing of Stalin's agents [excepting those previously identified] culled from an intercepted memo from Anatoly Gorsky, the KGB's resident agent operating out of DC Embassy:

Allan Rosenberg - Foreign Economic Administration

Bella Gold - Department of Commerce

Bernard Redmont - State Department

Charles Flato - Farm Security Administration

Charles Kramer - National Youth Administration, later Senate Staffer to the LaFollette Subcommittee of the Senate on Civil Liberties. Reputed to have run the Soviet spy ring called Mole, his wife, Christina was also a Soviet agent.

David Weintraub - UN Relief and Rehabilitation Administration

Donald Hiss - Department of Interior

Donald Wheeler - OSS & State Department

Duncan Lee - OSS

Edward Gitzgerald - Department of Commerce

F. V Reno, Aberdeen Proving Grounds

Frank Coe - Treasury Department

Franz Neumann - OSS & State Department

G. Silverman - Air Force

Gerald Graze - War Department

Gregory Silvermaster - Treasury Department

Harold Glasser - Treasury Department

Harry Bagdoff - Department of Commerce

Harry Dexter White - Treasury Department

Helen Tenney - OSS

Henry A. Wadleight [aka, Julian] State Deartment

Henry Collins, Department of Agriculture

Irving Kaplan - Treasury Department

Julius Joseph - OSS

Kudwig Ullman - War Department

Laurence Duggan - State Department

Lee Pressman, CIO

Maurice Halperin Oss & State Department

Noel Field, State Department

Robert Miller - State Department

Ruth Rivkin - UNRRA

Solomon Adler - Treasury Department

Sonia Gold - Treasury Department

Stanley Graze - OSS & State Department

V.V. Sveshnikov, War Department

Willard Park - State Department

William Remington - Department of Commerce

William W. Pigman - Bureau of Standards [source, Evans & Romerstein, pp. 101-102]

We cannot proceed beyond this point without understanding the idiosyncrasies of the Lend-Lease program, a hyper-critical wartime effort established to provide massive material aid to our allies. At first blush, this may sound entirely natural, the huge manufacturing capacity of the U.S. churning out ships, aircraft, munitions, vehicles, storehouses of food, even entire factories - much of which was being rationed at home - to aid our allies.

But there was a catch, as there always was when dealing with the "complex" relationship between Roosevelt and Stalin. A significant portion of this largesse was doled out to the Soviet Union under conditions that defy belief.

From the notes made by, arguably, the program's central player, an unpleasant truth emerges - that the Russian military was actively involved in directing the transfer of American property, industrial secrets and the most highly secured scientific information imaginable, including critical materials, to the USSR.

MAJOR GEORGE "RACEY" JORDAN FOR THE PROSECUTION

From our research it emerges that perhaps the key primary source of information on this and related topics are the diaries of Major George "Racey" Jordan, who had been assigned as a senior Lend-Lease liaison officer/expediter working in conjunction with the *Red Army Air Force*, first out of Newark, New Jersey's commercial airport and later stationed at the Great Falls AFB in Montana.

In just the first few pages it becomes clear that the Russian aspect of Lend Lease was operationally under the control of Roosevelt's body double, Harry Hopkins who very effectively became the Red's leading advocate, lobbyist and fixer. But in reading through Jordan's manuscript the level of subversion that FDR's people wrought on Americans would, if not documented as meticulously, be considered the product of some writer's over-active imagination.

To that end we have identified 10 key aspects demonstrating this claim, the entire document is available via an internet search:

1. By 1942 FDR had already committed the U.S., absent any legislative authority to membership in the United Nations, which was purportedly founded in October, 1945, thus proving his commitment to world government and a concomitant lack of devotion to the idea of U.S. sovereignty. This was counter to the public servant's oath of office "to protect and defend," as well as - in a constructive sense - extraordinarily unusual given that the U.S. was the sole superpower that emerged immediately post the great war.

It's striking to see the UN actually speaking for the U.S. in this time period.

"Joint Declaration by the United Nations, Washington, D.C., January 1, 1942, White House news release:

A Joint Declaration by The United States of America, The United Kingdom of Great Britain and Northern

Ireland, The Union of Soviet Socialist Republics, China, Australia, Belgium, Canada, Costa Rica, Cuba, Czechoslovakia, Dominican Republic, El Salvador, Greece, Guatemala, Haiti, Honduras, India, Luxembourg, Netherlands, New Zealand, Nicaragua, Norway, Panama, Poland..." [source, Major George "Racey" Jordan, From Major Jordan's Diaries, A Western Islands Book, Harcourt Brace, 1952, pg. 2]

2. Observations made by Major Jordan, that will be further documented later in this section, alleging that not only was the United States shipping uranium [the properties and even name of which were unknown to the public, as was its necessity to the success of the Manhattan Project, the most highly classified secret of the war] to the Soviet Union in direct contravention to any conception of state security, as well as the terms of Lend-Lease, it was pushed through the "pipeline" by none other than FDR's co-president, Harry Hopkins, the Director Of Lend-Lease:

Testimony - "Donald T. Appell, former F.B.I. agent and the special investigator for the Committee on Un-American Activities...

Mr. Nixon: Is it the intention of the staff, then, to present the witness [Victor A. Kravchenko] who may be able to substantiate, at least in part, Major Jordan's testimony that secret material was going through?

Mr. Appell: That is correct. [Mr. Kravchenko's testimony is quoted on pages 257-67]

Mr. Nixon: On the point of the so-called shipments of uranium, the shipments went through. Is that correct?

Mr. Appell: Two specific shipments of uranium oxide and uranium nitrate and shipments of heavy water have been completely documented to include even the number of the plane that flew the uranium and heavy water to Great Falls.

Mr. Nixon: And the final point is the matter of Mr. Hopkins having attempted to expedite the shipments. Major Jordan's testimony on that was that his notes, written at the time, showed the initials "H.H." on one of the consignments which he broke into. Your investigation has shown no correspondence of Mr. Hopkins in which he used the initials "H.H." Is that correct?

Mr. Appell: Yes." [pg.8]

3. A second attestation regarding FDR's intent to subordinate U.S. sovereignty to a global governmental entity that had not yet been recognized. But where had Kotikov gained his authority? Clearly the policy of giving the Soviets a great deal of authority regarding Lend-Lease, working through "the Big Boss," Harry Hopkins, could only have originated from within the Oval Office.

"I had met Colonel Kotikov [head of the Soviet mission at the commercial airfield] only a few days before, when I reported for duty on May 10, 1942. My orders gave the full title of the Newark base as "United Nations Depot No. 8, Lend-Lease Division, Newark Airport, Newark, New Jersey, International Section, Air Service Command, Air Corps, U.S. Army" [pg. 10]

4. Demonstrative of the new political hierarchy, after the Soviets had become inexplicably and wildly upset after having one of "their" airplanes [inarguably, still American property sitting on the tarmac of a major American airport] slightly damaged by a commercial aircraft, and despite assurance by Jordan that this presented no difficulty since it could be fixed while still meeting deadlines, Kotikov became nearly crazed in his degree of rage and immediately went over Jordan's head directly to the top, to Hopkins:

"I noticed that Colonel Kotikov was fidgeting scornfully. When I finished, he made an abrupt gesture with his hand. "I call Mr. Hopkins," he announced...[Jordan] What did Harry Hopkins have to do with Newark Airport?...[Kotikov] Mr. Hopkins fix...[he subsequently called the Soviet Embassy in DC]... Kotikov began a long harangue over the phone in Russian, interrupted by several trips to the window. The only words I understood were "American Airlines," "Hopkins," and the serial number on the tail...[Jordan]... That, I felt sure, was the end of the affair. I was wrong. On June 12th the order came from Washington not only ordering American Airlines off the field, but directing every aviation company to cease activities at Newark forthwith. The order was not for a day or a week. It held for the duration of the war, though they called it a "Temporary Suspension." I was flabbergasted. It was the sort of thing one cannot quite believe, and certainly cannot forget. Would we have to jump whenever Colonel Kotikov cracked the whip? For me, it was going to be a hard lesson to learn." [pg.11]

Speaking to the nature of Hopkins' allegiance:

"Harry Hopkins came to New York to address a Russian Red Rally at Madison Square Gardens. He cried: "A second front? "Yes, and if necessary, a third and a fourth front . . . The American people are bound to the people of the Soviet Union in the great alliance of the United Nations. They know that in the past year you have in your heroic combat against our common foe performed for us and for all humanity a service that can never be repaid. "We are determined that nothing shall stop us from sharing with you all that we have and are in this conflict, and we look forward to sharing with you the fruits of victory and peace."

Hopkins concluded: "Generations unborn will owe a great measure of their freedom to the unconquerable power of the Soviet people." [pg.13]

5. Jordan's first reference to uranium transshipments to Stalin:

"At this time I knew nothing whatever about the atomic bomb. The words "uranium" and "Manhattan Engineering District" were unknown to me. But I became aware that certain folders were being held to one side on Colonel Kotikov's desk for the accumulation of a very special chemical plant. In fact, this chemical plant was referred to by Colonel Kotikov as a "bomb powder" factory. *By referring to my diary, and checking the items I now know went into an atomic energy plant*, [emphasis added] I am able to show the following records starting with the year 1942, while I was still at Newark. These materials, which are necessary for the creation of atomic pile, moved to Russia in 1942:

Graphite: natural, flake, lump or chip, costing American taxpayers $812,437.

Over thirteen million dollars' worth of aluminum tubes (used in the atomic pile to "cook" or transmute the uranium into plutonium), the exact amount being $13,041,152...

We sent 834,989 pounds of cadmium metal for rods to control the intensity of an atomic pile; the cost was $781,472. The really secret material, thorium, finally showed up and started going through immediately. The amount during 1942 was 13,440 pounds at a cost of $22,848...On Jan. 30, 1943 we shipped an additional 11,912 pounds of thorium nitrate to Russia from Philadelphia on the S.S. John C. Fremont." [pg. 16-17]

6.   Jordan detailing the nonexistent control of "immigrating" Soviet personnel, showing the ease with which Stalin was seeding the country with Red spies:

"One really disturbing fact which brought this home to me was that the entry of Soviet personnel into the United States was completely uncontrolled. Planes were arriving regularly from Moscow with unidentified

Russians aboard. I would see them jump off planes, hop over fences, and run for taxicabs. They seemed to know in advance exactly where they were headed, and how to get there. It was an ideal set-up for planting spies in this country, with false identities, for use during and after the war...Major General Follette Bradley, USAF (Ret.), winner of the Distinguished Service Medal for his pioneering of the Alsib Pipeline, wrote in the New York times on Aug. 31, 1951:

"Of my own personal knowledge I know that beginning early in 1942 Russian civilian and military agents were in our country in large numbers." [pg. 37]

7. So great was Kotikov's influence that he, realizing that Jordan, then a Captain would have far greater authority if he were promoted to a higher military rank, petitioned the base's commanding officer to bust Jordan up a few pegs. It didn't take long for this novel method of promotion to occur:

"...He is much hindered in his good work by under rank with these officers who he asks for things all time. I ask you to recommend him for equal rank to help Russian movement here..."

8. It was at this time that - now Major - Jordan had begun, with alarm, to take note of the rapidly increasing number of packages that travelled under diplomatic immunity, from his then station in Great Falls, Montana to Moscow. This was clearly Soviet intelligence material that had been gathered in the United States that Uncle Joe wanted to see:

"...the unusual number of black patent-leather suitcases, bound with white window sash cord and sealed with red wax, which were coming through on the route to Moscow...The first black suitcases, six in number, were in charge of a Russian officer and I passed them without question upon his declaration that they were "personal luggage." But the units mounted to ten, twenty and thirty and at last to standard batches of fifty which weighed almost two tons and consumed the cargo allotment of an entire plane. The officers were replaced by armed couriers, traveling in pairs, and the excuse for avoiding inspection was changed from "personal luggage" to "diplomatic immunity." Here were tons of materials proceeding to the Soviet Union, and I had no idea what they were…" [pg.38]

9. Jordan, taking the initiative proceeded to, at an early point in these transactions, examine the contents of 18 sealed black suitcases out of the now standard shipment of 50 at a time - the entire space usually allotted in a cargo shipment. What he found, this author still finds amazing in scope and audacity. Jordan noted that when he expressed an intent to spot check the contents of the packages the Soviet personnel minding them, "were half-mad with fury and terror." So unglued were the Ruskies that Jordan thought they might shoot him - they all carried pistols in shoulder holsters, as if one needed to compound the craziness that was already present. The Major's orders were clear, ordering a nearby GI that if the Commies drew their weapons to drop them. Dutifully the soldier chambered a round in his rifle and stuck the muzzle into the cargo bay:

"in the back I found a series of tables listing railroad mileages from almost any point in the United States to any other….[and]…scores of roadmaps, of the sort available at filling stations to all comers…Taken together, they furnished a country-wide chart, with names and places, of American industrial plants…Another was filled with documents relating to the Aberdeen Proving Ground, one of the most "sensitive" areas in the war effort…Other folders were stuffed with naval and shipping intelligence. There seemed to be hundreds of commercial catalogues and scientific magazines. I noted that there were letters from Yakov M. Lomakin. Afterwards, as Soviet Consul General in New York, he played a part in the Mme. Kasenkina "leap for freedom" incident which forced him to quit the country. There were also sheafs of information about Mexico, Argentina and Cuba…all such papers had been trimmed close to the text, with white margins removed. I decided this was done either to save weight, or to remove "Secret," "Confidential" or "Restricted" stamps that might have halted a shipment, or for both reasons. I distinctly remember five or six State Department folders, bound with stout rubber bands. Clipped to each was a tab. The first read: "From Sayre." I took down the words because it ran through my head that someone of that name had recently been High Commissioner to the Philippines. Then I copied the legend: *"From Hiss."* [pg.41-42]

That would be Alger Hiss, perhaps the most publicly infamous member of the Soviet spy operation and an Assistant to the Assistant Secretary of State...for trade agreements.

How convenient, the right guy, the right time at the right place as his Soviet masters had intended.

10. In April, 1943 Kotikov asked if there was room in the already backlogged shipments to fast-track a very special 2,000 pound container. Jordan, informed him that no, it would not be possible since they were already really far behind.

Hold on to your hats...

Kotikov asked Jordan to put a call through to DC. After the connection had been made and after he had finished conversing with someone in Russian, he turned to Jordan:

"Big boss, Mr. Hopkins, wants you." It was quite a moment, I was about to speak for the first time with a legendary figure of the day, the top man in the world of Lend-Lease in which I lived. I have been careful to keep the following account as accurate in substance and language as I can...A bit in awe I stammered, "Jordan speaking." A male voice began at once: "This is Mr. Hopkins. Are you my expediter out there?" I answered that I was the United Nations Representative at Great Falls, working with Colonel Kotikov. "Did you get those pilots I sent you?" "Oh yes, sir," I responded. "They were very much appreciated, and helped us in unblocking the jam in the Pipeline. We were accused of going out of channels, and got the dickens for it." Mr. Hopkins let that one go by, and moved on to the heart of things. "Now, Jordan," he said, "there's a certain shipment of chemicals going through that I want you to expedite. This is something very special." "Shall I take it up," I asked, "with the Commanding Colonel?"

"I don't want you to discuss this with anyone," Mr. Hopkins ordered, "and it is not to go on the records. Don't make a big production of it, but just send it through quietly, in a hurry."[emphasis added]

Thus was demonstrated the organizational structure and power relationships of the new command. It was the brass of the Russian Air Force who were calling the shots on an American program in which billions of dollars of hardware and other materials were transferred to their regime, gratis, and that Roosevelt's body-double, Hopkins, functioned as Stalin's pet expediter, not that he was in any way unwilling.

Cognitive dissonance...

Though evidence of the Soviet's influence peddling operation existed everywhere the administration had set up shop; what remains startling was how far up FDR's chain of command an unapologetic and freely expressed treasonous mindset had risen.

Reflect upon a statement made by the star of Mission to Moscow, the former United States ambassador, Joseph E. Davies was quoted in a Washington Times-Herald article, dated February 18, 1946 as saying:

"Russia, in self-defense, has every moral right to seek atomic bomb secrets through military espionage, if excluded from such information from her former allies." [pg. 51]

Keep in mind that the Rosenbergs were fried for carrying out Davies' suggested policy.

In another example of how history oddly seems to pair events, only two weeks later [May 5, 1946] - noting the brutal oppression that the Soviets were already imposing on Eastern Europe - that Winston Churchill made his famous, "Iron Curtain" speech at Westminster College, Fulton, Missouri:

> "It is my duty however, for I am sure you would wish me to state the facts as I see them to you, to place before you certain facts about the present position in Europe. *From Stettin in the Baltic to Trieste in the Adriatic, an iron curtain has descended across the Continent.* [emphasis added] Behind that line lie all the capitals of the ancient states of Central and Eastern Europe. Warsaw, Berlin, Prague, Vienna, Budapest, Belgrade, Bucharest and Sofia, all these famous cities and the populations around them lie in what I must call the Soviet sphere"

Hoping to provide a palpable sense of how brazenly the Soviets had been working with traitorous members of the Roosevelt administration, the following summary will yield an additional and expanded account - relying on the records about which only Jordan and the Russian partners - who had been forced upon him - were aware, just how much critical atomic bomb making material Hopkins and we must assume at some level Roosevelt, had provided to what was by this time clearly the Red Menace, regardless of the state of denial that Congressional Democrats were in at the time and how this entire matter has been subsequently buried by servile leftist historians such as Howard Zinn.

Grouped under the heading "Atomic materials," was the following:

Uranium metal 2.2 lbs., a truly staggering amount, since at the time it represented about half of the entire U.S.

stockpile, making its value beyond measure, perhaps approaching $1 billion[!] given the extraordinarily high-tech nature [and cost] of the Manhattan Project which the U.S. had created to produce it.

Additionally there were 806,941 lbs of cobalt metal/cobalt-bearing scrap [valued at, $1,190,774] - 9,681 lbs of beryllium [$10,874] - 72,535 lbs of cadmium alloys [$70,029] - 834,989 lbs of cadmium metals [$71,466] - 33,600 lbs cobalt [$49,782] - [pg. 75-76]

The manifest continues on and on, the sense of shock being amplified with each revelation...

Even in the least malign reading, the breadth, detail and uncontested nature of this information presents the picture of a president oblivious to the most basic elements of maintaining national security during the most destructive war in history. This is aside from what can only kindly be called a "logic gap," as he gaily went about facilitating the Soviet infiltration of America and the subsequent subversion of the Free World.

The administration might as well have presented Stalin with the A-bomb wrapped as a glow in the dark matryoshka.

Though this aspect of the overall critique could be considered case closed, the story does not end there...not by a long shot if we hope to approach a fuller appreciation of the origin of the Deep State.

Synopsizing, we trust that those who might have been a little unclear regarding this period in history now understand that Stalin was anything but an ally, let alone a friend and that the Soviets only became our war "partner" due to events beyond their control. What was entirely avoidable, however, was Roosevelt's cavalier approach to preserving the integrity of the society that had showered so much material comfort and fame upon his family.

Regardless of how skillfully exculpatory language might be constructed, it remains undeniable that previous to our new "relationship," Hitler and Stalin had partnered in carving up Poland - tigers on a tethered goat - in 1939. This rapacious pairing continued until 1941, only ending when an over-confident, egomaniacal Hitler violated the secret Molotov-Ribbentrop non-aggression pact and opened an Eastern Front attacking his former partner in genocide as part of Operation Barbarossa, to which Hitler committed over 150 divisions, 19 of which were mechanized, i.e., Panzer armies.

Though it is accurate that the Russian people fought the Nazis with the kind of bravery and ferocity that is legendary in defense of Stalingrad, the guy pulling the strings...and stacking the corpses with abandon [Soviet casualties in all stages of the offensive hovered near 1M] relied on American hardware to repulse the attack and subsequently drive hard into the bosom of Europe, as Diana West wryly notes, behind the wheel of "Dodge trucks."

Through its clever manipulation of an apparently willing FDR, his closest confidants and the moles nested within the new federal agencies, the Soviets were able to get exactly what they wanted, which extended far beyond material needs.

The Soviet network and resulting influence peddling was so effective that it was able to actually dictate some of the most sensitive of America's strategic decisions.

In this regard Stalin's expectations, based upon his prior successes were high, so much so that he alternatively hectored then demanded that the Allies "open a second" front in the war. *This was at a time when a second front had already been established by the Allies* - by necessity - that in the Far East, targeting Imperial Japan after the December 1941 Pearl Harbor attack. Not surprisingly, he had no interest in joining this effort, being a "one" front kind of guy.

Let's explore this subject a little more deeply because it really sets the table for what happened after the Axis Powers had been defeated.

The opening gambit, or first front for the Allies had been the North African campaign fought in and around Tunisia and from that foot-hold, the invasion of Italy. One of the strategic objectives here was the desire to make the Mediterranean navigable again, which would have been a huge boon to allied shipping much of which had been deployed to the Far East theater where the German U-boat wolf-packs sent tens of thousands of naval and merchant marine personnel to their deaths

Churchill was the primary political leader supporting this plan. He was eventually outmaneuvered by Hopkins who had apparently convinced the president to side with Stalin's demand that the "second front" originate in Western Europe.

It was no secret that the president was not fond of Churchill, a petty sentiment that he allowed to color his every dealing with the PM. While FDR displayed a typically "progressive" and simplistic contempt for the United Kingdom which historically had been grounded in a rather benevolent form of colonialism, irony seemed to be totally wasted on the 32nd president, whose actions guaranteed that the USSR would be free to brutally "colonize" half of Europe…with his blessing.

Be that as it may, and feuds aside, also sensing the impending danger posed by an ascendant Stalin and the promise of the Mediterranean strategy, the English PM had an early ally in General Eisenhower [who also was eventually pressured into opposing the move…much intrigue there] and the commander of the invasion of Sicily, General Mark Clark who also saw the Italian campaign in Churchill's expansive terms.

Churchill, Clark and Eisenhower reasoned that invading Europe, from its Africa stronghold via Italy would serve two purposes. The first being that the Allies had already committed a huge number of troops in furtherance of the campaign which succeeded in routing the Nazis in Italy and therefore were naturally pre-staged to press northward. The second - anathema to FDR, Hopkins and Stalin, again that troubling constituency - was that if that pathway was allowed to serve as the access point for the general invasion of Europe, the Americans and Brits would likely have been able to accomplish two goals that in hindsight would have changed the history of the modern world. It would have allowed the Allied forces to beat the Reds to Germany as well as - and this was Stalin's greatest fear - assume blocking positions against the westward expansion of the Soviets who were beleaguered after finally repulsing the Nazis in the Russian winter were temperatures hovered at around 40 degrees below zero.

Geopolitical considerations came into play here as Churchill and top level American foreign policy professionals such as Ambassador William Bullitt were entirely clear-headed and understandably fearful that as the Red Army broke the siege of Stalingrad and moved into Easter Europe, they were preparing the way for the eventual subjugation of that entire region after the war had been concluded in the West.

This suggested new order of battle - driven by a far more realistic and hence, sober assessment of Soviet aims - was not-so-surprisingly rejected by FDR and Stalin, the fraternal tag-team who had made the decision that the "second" front be launched across the English Channel into France thereby making it impossible to stop Stalin, assuming there was ever such an intent by FDR...factual material in support of such a conclusion being nonexistent.

As a result, troops that had been assigned to the Italian/Mediterranean invasion plan were taken out of the fight and assigned to what eventually became Operation Overlord. Additionally a great number of divisions had already been held in the reserve for the planned invasion of France and hence unavailable for the Italian campaign.

We know the rest of the sorry history...

The threat clear, the Allies occupied themselves with taking down the Imperial Japanese knowing that it would end the war, but because of the tremendous influence that Stalin was able to wield, the U.S. and its partners unbelievably had maneuvered themselves into a position where it became impossible [even if there had been the will] to prevent the Soviet gangster from doing what everyone knew he had in mind, grabbing as much of Germany as possible and then one by one picking off the Eastern European countries.

Most assuredly the Iron Curtain had fallen.

As heretofore referenced, the dire prediction that the Soviets would likely do this was meticulously laid out mid-war by the long-time U.S. major foreign policy player, former Ambassador to the USSR [who was followed by Davies] William C. Bullitt, in a single spaced,15 page hand-typed briefing to FDR in January of 1943:

> "[referring to Stalin's post-war aims]…He may set up Soviet governments in many of the countries in which we now expect to set up democratic government. We have little first hand, detailed information about Stalin's views and aims…It may be that Stalin having "liquidated" the old communist to whom Communism was a religion, having been shocked by the consequences of his own collaboration with Hitler, having probed [as we can't] the depth of the wound inflicted on the Soviet Union by Hitler's armies…it may be that Stalin, chastened, has changed. The persons who hold this to be true say that we can obtain Stalin's full and frank cooperation, if only we [basically give everything that Stalin is demanding, which literally was everything]…They say that Stalin will trust us and work with us hand-in-hand, if we trust him and give him these things…This view of Stalin is not only the view of several recent travelers in the Soviet Union but also the view being propagated by the Comintern. It is the communist party line in Great Britain, the United State and all other countries where there are communist parties. It is the line of fellow travelers and many "liberals." Since Stalin personally sets the party line, it is what Stalin wants us to believe

about him...*The most careful search for factual evidence to support the thesis that Stalin is a changed man reveals none...*" Emphasis added [source, William C. Bullitt, *Secret Memorandum to FDR* dated January 29, 1943, pp. 2-3, Yale University, William C. Bullitt Archives].

The harsh reality was, at the "end" of the war the West was arguably worse off than it had been before.

In the case of the United States, the Commander In Chief had to deliver the most heart-rending message a parent will ever receive, to the families of the 416,000 young Americans whose lives had been sacrificed, not to overlook the over 1M souls who perished in Britain and France.

All wars are brutal, gristly affairs, but sometimes they are unavoidable as was the case with the American entry into World War II, but at the cessation of hostilities, the political leadership has to be held to account in order to justify the loss.

What did it yield?

Abstract:

I. Europe, materially scarred and psychically damaged; though Britain was undoubtedly still British, broke and deprived of empire it was no longer "Great." Pointing to today's low-growth Continental societies as evidence to the contrary reflects a willful blindness to the darkness that lurks beneath the veneer, a festering sore that knows no relief.

II. In a brief span of time the Allies had lost the flower of their culture, their youth, especially their then still tough, masculine young men. Neither species nor societies are well served by killing off their alpha-males - but in Europe, and to a lesser degree in America, this happened twice within a single generation. The Brits lost 740,00 and the French over 1M in the First World War, America, a late comer to the conflict, suffered over 50,000 killed in action - all to an armistice that seemed entirely designed to lead them

53

inexorably into the next conflict, the worst in mankind's history. Looking back it could be likened to harvesting prize live stock, waiting till the next generation had sufficiently matured then killing off the lot of them.

III. Emotional devastation wrought from the Atlantic, to the Mediterranean to the Black Sea. Shattered peoples and political systems, that in one of the most ironic aspects of modern history, rapidly took on the major attributes of the socialism that so many millions had just died to cast off.

IV. It was with an ill-considered popular mandate - borne of a sense of hopelessness and the natural human desire for personal security - that governments became ever bigger and more intrusive to the point of creating a level of dependency previously unimaginable. It didn't take long for many of the serfs so minted to realize that they had little of value worth protecting, their lives shallow. Who could have then foreseen that all too soon the nature of their lives, including the "inalienable" rights that the West embraced, would be controlled by a bunch of faceless, unelected bureaucrats in a city [Brussels] located in an inconsequential, tiny little country [Belgium] that many could not even locate on a map.

V. These people mined the emotional wreckage after years of all out warfare so devastating that it stripped them of their faith, materially changing the way the European nation states thought about themselves. Consequently, difficult to grasp concepts such as sovereignty which had been developed hundreds of years previous [the Treaty of Westphalia, 1648, that ended the Thirty Years War] thoroughly escaped them.

VI. In large part this was the start of the process where today we see so much of the cultural confidence of the West being sapped. The absolute devastation led to citizens questioning the basic goodness and exceptionalism of their own societies, the great achievements of the Enlightenment, the Reformation, Industrial Revolution, scientific discoveries, the arts...all of which were cast aside, rendering a once proud people psychologically ill-equipped to resist the very aggressive and supremely culturally confident onslaught of the Islamic hijrah.

VII. On this side of the pond, in short order America had also been changed beyond recognition, now encumbered by a massive bureaucracy with an expansive authority and newly developed powers of taxation. Adding considerably to this mix, America was witness to a rapidly evolving media firmly under the control of the left.

VIII. Most poignantly, after years of total mobilization amidst the bloodshed, sorrow and unbelievable heroism, the world had been...but of course...made safe for Stalin to display the treachery that had been his key personality trait since he brutally crushed Soviet Georgia in 1922 - against the wishes of Lenin - whose grip on the nation was slipping.

FDR sided with his Red pal, Uncle Joe, until America's longest serving president died at the very beginning of his fourth term. Once again we are reminded that there is no cosmic sense of justice, in this case FDR had never been forced to confront the consequences of his imperious foolishness. Nonetheless it is hard to imagine under any circumstance how his actions could ever have been justified when contrasted against the forces that had been loosed upon the world which steadily and unrelentingly gnawed at the spiritual foundation of Western greatness.

Probing a bit deeper, the influence operation having proven entirely successful, Stalin got even more than he had hoped for. Precisely as Ambassador Bullitt had predicted, to the degree that Stalin's advances were met with indecision, he proceeded with even greater vigor.

Roosevelt's policies and those made around him in the haze of his failing health, were the equivalent of dispatching a life boat to save the drowning tyrant instead of what should have happened, the Nazis and Soviets being encouraged to annihilate each other in the abattoir of the dark Soviet winter, snakes entwined in the ultimate danse macabre.

Instead, Roosevelt and his subversive infested government had taken a bedridden Soviet state, propped it up, shot it full of penicillin and then facilitated its march into Berlin...and beyond.

Though the bombs stopped falling and birds were once again heard singing, the military and psychological devastation in Europe would dictate a new reality. As we would shortly learn, the cessation of hostilities would only apply to the shooting war, because the ravenous Soviet Bear having come out of hibernation was once again on the prowl.

Perhaps worst of all, thanks to Roosevelt's willful blindness, the Marxist proto-state had been allowed to establish deep roots in America. So the reality behind the confetti was quite different, as amidst oddly hollow victory parades, joyful newspaper headlines and mad embraces of returning servicemen, the conflict merely shifted gears and continued to grind on in the form of a 50 year long, nuclear-tipped Cold War.

That pathway would be littered by constant and poorly fought, hot flash-wars of "national liberation" accompanied by budget busting expenditure of countless trillions of dollars on defensive measures that shouldn't have been necessary.

But wait, many will ask at this point, didn't the "good guys" prevail, weren't the Soviets ultimately defeated?

Perhaps, but if so, it was an odd and bitter peace because at this point we must revisit our central thesis, as the genuine - as opposed to the idealized - historical facts have now been established with enough clarity to resolve the once hazy larger picture.

If one adopts the more precise heuristic of peace being more than the absence of kinetic conflict, then there was no cause to rejoice. Instead the war was merely tidied up, institutionalized within the mandate of a new class of collectivist Western autocratic managers who relentlessly drove the cultural Marxist narrative into an emerging designer culture heavy on paternalism, an ever expanding bureaucratic state and the gem really, control of a lush but new and alien information highway - the Deep State had arisen.

We are the children of that transformation. Though having had no say in the matter, hopefully, due to our now corrected historical revisionism we have gained a much greater appreciation for the new power dynamic while observing how forcefully the Deep State is now moving to control the process in which culture and information are married.

Quite recently, July, 2017, Google made the decision to radically redesign its news delivery algorithm. Abandoning the legacy format - with many outbound links on a wide variety of topics vertically stacked and available on the splash page - Google's "product" is now heavily curated with an absurdly hard-left bias. Now, since the company actually "tells" you how to think about the news and what the "top stories" are, the re-coded matrix resembles the journalistic equivalent of an anti-Trump/alt-Right lynching..

For example, during the late morning of July 25, 2017 the following is what a news consumer would see in the first few lines at news.google.com:

- Trump escalates shame campaign against Sessions
- Rumors abound about other imminent White House firings and resignations
- Trump's gratuitously political Boy Scouts speech, annotated
- Trump's Boy Scouts speech broke with 80 years of presidential tradition
- Trump goes on wild riff to Boy Scouts about a real estate developer and a party with 'the hottest people in New York'
- Trump leaves Sessions twisting in the wind while berating him publicly
- Highly Cited· Washington Post - Is Trump Trying to "Throw the Attorney General of the United States Overboard?"

- Donald J. Trump on Twitter: "Attorney General Jeff Sessions has taken a VERY weak position on Hillary Clinton crimes
- The GOP's Insane "Pass Something" Plan

This is far beyond heavy-handed; it is weaponized media, coordinated fire directed against an agreed upon target, in this case the President of the United States.

Clearly, Google/Alphabet's big bosses have established a new American peerage system, the globalist princes of Silicon Valley. Jousting for similar recognition are the principals at Facebook, Twitter, Linkedin, Pinterest, etc., followed a host of lesser dukes making it a defining issue of the time.

In the second example we turn to YouTube - surprise - a Google company - actually most of the Google-verse has been folded into the aforementioned Alphabet holding company. For some time the video service has been selectively "culling" and removing loops it deems as containing "offensive material."

Anyone who has read this far now should recognize, the technique of censorship under the false flag of a claimed, but nonexistent morality is one of the cultural Marxist's most powerful tools.

As of this writing YouTube is aggressively suspending accounts [or hiding and thus "demonetizing" channels] featuring content that has been deemed offensive. There is no avenue of appeal; the decisions are simply made and the affected party has little recourse. Given the paucity of information currently available, we can only guess what is going on behind the electrons. We do however know the code-words, Islamophobic, alt-Right, racist, hateful and the like, all of which sublimate to expressing viewpoints the Deep Staters views as threatening.

Consider the net effect on the free flow of information when YouTube's definition of "Islamophobia" becomes identical to the legalism of Shari'a based, Islamic, blasphemy laws...the

Internet monopolists are acting in the role of all-powerful electronic jihadist imams bent upon the anti-Western notion of enforced Shari'a compliance. It's probably no great surprise that hateful videos placed by jihadist/AntiFa/Marxist groups don't seem to engender the same level of "outrage."

Necessary digression aside, back to the historical timeline.

On The Warpath - Taking Scalps

Though in fact America had been significantly restructured over previous decades, it's hard to argue that the symbolic passing of the republic to the internal enemy took place during the late 60s and early 70s.

From 1965 to 1968 the Marxist, Students for a Democratic Society [SDS] became the face of the Democrat Party, all the while developing the ideology for its domestic terror wing - the Weathermen and then, with the FBI hot on their trail, the Weather Underground: Bill Ayers, Bernardine Dohrn, Diana Oughton, Terry Robbins Ted Gold, Kathy Boudin and Cathy Wilkerson, etc.

1968 was the pivotal year; the hard-left rioted at the scene of the Democratic Convention, especially in Chicago's Grant Park, resulting in the federal prosecution of the ringleaders, the "Chicago 7" - Abbie Hoffman, Tom Hayden, Jerry Rubin, David Dellinger, Rennie Davis, John Froines, and Lee Weiner.

In less than a decade it was people of this ilk who were firmly in command of the Democrat Party.

Developing this thesis a bit more, though self-described as the "New Left" it was more on the order of a forced changing of the guard with the old lefties being shoved aside, in a manner very reminiscent of Stalin's purging of the very loyal but now superfluous and possibly politically dangerous, "old Bolsheviks," by newly minted, highly educated, angry and quite politically gifted Marxists.

The new guard was so firmly in command that even though America remained outwardly patriotic and traditional - space launches being watched with amazement and pride in most grammar and high schools - the modern enemies of the West presented such a poisonous digression that they were able within the space of 6 years, claim the scalps of two presidents, effectively decapitating the old-line Dems as well as the GOPers, who true to form expended little energy by way of resistance.

The first kill-shot targeted the war-consumed Democrat, President Lyndon Johnson who seeing his country wracked with civil unrest arising out of long simmering ethnic tensions as well the massive anti-war protests took himself out of the 1968 election cycle, knowing that he had been rendered a divisive force.

The second of these silent coups took place in 1974 when President Richard Nixon was forced to step down after the events surrounding the Watergate affair. In this matter, as is the case today, the GOP simply rolled over and refused to fight, leaving Nixon with no reasonable alternative.

Both of these actions were adroitly executed with an almost military level of precision, with public relations being handled by an intensely smug, monopoly electronic media - the "three big" broadcast networks, ABC, CBS and NBC.

Thus the news delivery business had become an arm of the DNC, working in collusion with its leftist counterparts in the New York and Washington DC press.

As was the case with President GW Bush during the Afghan and Iraqi wars, Johnson was pilloried every day in bold 72 point type "above the fold" headlines that screamed 30...35...40 thousand young American soldiers had been killed in a war that few seemed to understand for what it was, a proxy war, initiated by Mao's Red China. It is often said that it was CBS' chief anchor Walter Cronkite who forced both the U.S. out of South Vietnam as well as LBJ from the White House.

The exit of Nixon was greased a bit, preceded by the left's first strategic leak of the era, leading to the 1971 New York Times publishing excerpts of a highly classified report - the official, desanitized history of the Vietnam War - after it had been stolen by a defense analyst Daniel Ellsberg who worked for the RAND intelligence consulting firm.

Decapitating two successive presidencies was historically unprecedented and the net effect was to intensify the already deep rifts that were coursing through the society. The success of these actions also served to embolden and strengthen the relationship between the two key players, the radicalized Democrat Party and the equally defiant American media.

Wanting to become the "Don" of this Casa Nostra like organization, the Democrats made an extremely bold move against Big Intel that resulted in them being able to claim a third battle tropy; this one having been lifted by Senator Frank Church [D-ID] in 1975 as chair of the United States Senate Select Committee to Study Governmental Operations with Respect to Intelligence Activities that went after the CIA hammer and tong [in but a single explosive example charging the spy agency with assassinating foreign leaders] in choreographed public sessions, a very effective shot across the bow.

Riding on such a zephyr-like head wind the Marxist-Leninist element of the counter-culture had emerged as America's primary societal driver.

In hindsight it's clear what had transpired; since the old communist cell structure had been designed for another era, its basic attributes were repurposed into a more virulent [and nuanced] matrix. It is this complexly constructed entity that has sucked the United States, and actually the entirety of Western Civilization, into what could well be the final global conflict - an undeclared civil war pitting Stalin's heirs and the class-struggle, structural analysis, critical theory, etc., organizational principles of the Marxist left, against the forces of classical liberalism.

For want of the West, civilization was lost.

Though the landscape is much changed, the goals of the left remain the same, total domination of the culture and the obliteration of ordered liberty.

THEORY MEETS REALITY

The preceding section, compressed as it is we hope has retold the history of the previous century to accurately document the hidden reality of a society under external and internal ideological attack, by what used to be cavalierly dismissed by the cognoscenti as the "Red Baiters" and practitioners of "McCarthyism."

Though the Soviet Union no longer exists, the American left has for strategic reasons, adopted a position 180 degree out of phase with its historic partnership with the Evil Empire, now working overtime to cast Vladimir Putin as a modern day Stalin [when in actuality they used to adore the mustachioed, brutal killer of millions] who is merely a very bright, politically adept and Westernized hooligan, albeit one trained by the KGB.

Vlad no longer rules over an agrarian country populated by ignorant serfs but rather a hybridized system that more closely resembles a mafia-like state, comfortable with capitalistic enterprise...within limits which will not be allowed to be transgressed. Those who raise their heads too far in dissent tend to get the polonium cocktail treatment; these boys are still 100% Russian tough guys and play for keepskies.

In this blindingly quick metamorphosis, the left has gone from a very long period of cooperating with the Stalinist effort to dismantle traditional America to attacking a modern Russia that bears little resemblance to the USSR, inventing the meme of collusion between Putin and the President of the United States with the sole purpose of forcing him from office.

For the Deep State, the election of New York's "blonde barbarian" Trump, was the nightmare outlier [again, Taleb's Black Swan event] that was beyond its capacity to even imagine. But at around 9:30 EST on November the 8th, it became impossible to ignore the fact that the next President of the United States was a billionaire, genuinely alpha-male not beholden to the clubby political class and fearless in the face of institutional warfare.

Working towards a conclusion, there are three intellectual concepts that though dated, remain central to the perpetuation of the Marxist/progressive revolutionary movement, which has been redefined to reconcile the passion and techniques of the antiquarian Reds with their progeny who dominate today's college campuses, the legacy media and the other societal drivers that form the Deep State.

Thus noted, on April 9, 1917, Vladimir Lenin [an alias, having been born Ulyanov] had the following published, as a sort of official Op-Ed in the ever reliable newspaper, Pravda.

"What is this dual-power? Alongside the [bourgeoisie] Provisional Government...another government has arisen, weak and incipient, but undoubtedly a government that actually exists...the Soviets of Workers' and Soldiers' Deputies. What is the class composition of this other government? It consists of the proletariat and the peasants...What is the political nature of this government?...revolutionary dictatorship...power directly based on revolutionary seizure, on the direct initiative of the people from below, and not on a law enacted by a centralised state power. It is an entirely different kind of power from [that] which exists in the parliamentary bourgeois-democratic republics of...Europe and America." [V. I. Lenin Pravda No. 28, The Dual-power..." [source, Marxists Internet Archive]

In pre-revolutionary settings the need for "dual-power" quickly becomes apparent - the first cancer cell dividing.

Since the violent seizure of the Russian government itself did not occur until October and there already existed a provisional, though floundering governing body led by PM Kerensky, Lenin's dual-power served as a kind of springboard of sorts for his end-game, a totalitarian dictatorship which was not fully in place until the end of the Russian Civil War [1918-1922].

In Russia, despite Marx, Engels' and Lenin's claimed inevitability of a bottom-up worker's revolution, it was nowhere in evidence. Certainly there was the stoking of general societal unrest with the instigation of labor strikes and their effect was potentiated by the natural dislocation that was a consequence of the earlier abdication of Tsar Nicholas, yet there was no organic communist uprising. Thus the Bolsheviks realized the depressing fact that even a people with a very long history of having been victimized by totalitarian regimes would prove resistant to the direction that Marxism-Leninism had predicted - it would require the imposition of force.

This represented a fatal intellectual contradiction to the theoretical basis of the ideology.

Lenin of course realizing this, quickly proffering that the worker's revolution had been "temporarily" stymied by capitalism, it having been refined to the point where the "division of labor" had became the norm. The nuance of Lenin's argument was far more complex but it's not necessary to further tease it out for our purposes.

What was important was that though fallacious in nature, it was a defense nonetheless, around which could be built a reassuring narrative. However it was not until the 1930s that the whole idea of a "class struggle" based "dictatorship of the proletariat" could again become relevant, this time through a wholesale reinterpretation, rendering a disproven intellectual theory into a very effective process.

The person offering this salvific idea was the Italian Marxist theorist of the early 20th century, Antonio Gramsci. Though he very much agreed with Lenin and the need for "dual-power" there was a marked differentiation as to the interpretation of its nature if it was going to be effective.

To Lenin, the proto-state was something one built mechanically as political organizing historically had been done, choosing party members to serve in the various directorates of the mechanism, but Gramsci's insight was that unless the alternative state arose in a somewhat organic manner it would generally be resisted by a traditional culture. Inherent in this idea was the realization that communism could not rise of its own accord as the inevitable consequence of the unfolding of history [Marx's take on the Hegelian notion of historicism].

Seeing that the extant cultures resisted such an abrupt change he devised the methodology of slowly re-engineering the nature of Western society so it became more naturally receptive to the theory of Marxist revolutionary change. He called the process, "marching through the institutions" which envisioned a slow infiltration of the entities that created the prevailing society, the media, entertainment, education, literature and the arts, the political and judicial establishment etc., - in Gramsci's terminology, a new hegemony.

In assessing the general nature of today's society one must grant that the process does indeed work, today's overlords being the progeny of the decade between 1965 and 1975.

Thus instead of looking at the evidence: intersex bathrooms and showers, assertions of "white privilege" and the power of deconstructionist/intersectionalist analysis within the various fields of study which comprise the liberal arts, as being proof of societal insanity, it must be understood that while still pathological, these ideas more correctly bear the telltale traces of religious fanaticism, one produced by the sacralized ideology of a revised, Gramscian-influenced, Marxism-Leninism.

The ghost of Stalin still smiles smugly over the counter-culture he, and of course, FDR largely made possible.

But the left has more tools in its bag of revolutionary tricks, this one also courtesy of Uncle Joe. Since we now know the wisdom of rejecting the Deep State's smoke-screen "common knowledge death of the USSR" narrative, we see the Evil Empire as a more malign and effective ghostly presence.

Much like Islamism; though the prophet is gone the ideas, methods and motivational principles have with great purpose been brought into line with modernity.

There is demonstrable proof of this.

When one examines the wide-spread street violence that followed in the wake of November 8 [and even previous to that event going back to 2014 and Ferguson, MO] the hard hand of the leftist activists remain visible. The protests and riots in major American cities were in large part organized by the retrograde Stalinist left. The funding was provided by billionaire globalists such as George Soros, murky sources within Putin's Russia, the World Workers Party, former Lyndon Johnson AG Ramsey Clark's "above board" clone, the International Action Committee and its bastard Kamikaze child, International ANSWER/ANSWER Coalition, all of which partnered in the street-side heavy lifting [please refer to Kelly Riddell, *George Soros funds Ferguson protests, hopes to spur civil action - Liberal billionaire gave at least $33 million in one year to groups that emboldened activists*, Washington Times]

To move past this point with understanding, we now must consider the previously referenced, but ill-identified principle called "socialist realism."

Imagine looking at a snapshot and then removing everything that is inconsistent with a graphic depiction of the progressive world view. This then becomes the working leftist narrative despite the disjunctive relationship it has with what truly exists. Thus the struggle consists of constantly expanding a manufactured perception. Within this stylized view, everything that is at odds with this vision becomes, anathematized as "the enemy." Expanding into the realm of written language, it must be acknowledged that the progressives have displayed great skill in de-coupling the political lexicon from the actual meaning of language.

Non-binary gender?

Has this been lifted from "One Flew Over the Cuckoo's Nest" or perhaps the worlds-colliding, bar scene in "Star Wars"?

When one party has the uncontested ability to define words in whatever way is beneficial to its program, cultural manipulation is a given.

In a very recent case we look at the June 20, 2017 race in Georgia's 6th Congressional district between Republican Karen Handel and Democrat, John Ossoff. As we have come to expect in these matters, throughout the race the polls consistently showed that Ossoff was destined to win.

Reading the June 9 edition of the Atlanta Journal Constitution, the state's largest newspaper, would lead one to believe that Ossoff would win going away, having a seemingly insurmountable 7 point lead. Six weeks later though, the AJC didn't seem at all embarrassed to report that its darling [who didn't even live in the district] was crushed by Handel in a 5 point victory, a twelve point about-face.

Unless a candidate self-combusts during the last few weeks of a campaign, this is the sign of a sure fix, a newspaper actively manipulating its polling methodology, hoping to suppress GOP turnout.

Clearly, the paper was playing into the Democrat narrative as buoyed by nearly $30M dollars in outside-the-district contributions, primarily from the San Francisco Bay Area and the Burghers located an hour's drive to the South, in the area homesteaded by two of the true pioneers of the global village, William Hewlett and David Packard.

This is exactly how the process works, the story-line is arrived at by consensus within the Deep State; conference calls are arranged, at various times involving hundreds of reporters [see, Jonathan Strong, *The Fix was in: Journolist e-mails reveal how the liberal media shaped the 2008 election*, Daily Caller] to coordinate the ongoing coverage; polling is deliberately cooked then presented as news; raw copy is actually submitted to Democrat front-runners for approval, unbelievably even before hitting the editor's desk - all of which is presented as allegedly unbiased journalism.

The resultant Frankenstein's monster is then underwritten by the capitalism for us, socialism for you crowd, often those who star in Hollywood's mega-blockbusters. The linkage once forged, remains; the left stealthily controls Hollywood to a degree that would have been unimaginable in the 1940s.

Finally we wish to devote a few lines to an idea advanced by a critically important [though largely unremembered] Marxist, a German by the name of Herbert Marcuse who greatly influenced other socialist intellectuals such as Max Horkheimer in jointly developing the idea of "critical theory" as part of the "Frankfurt School," technically, Goethe University's Institute for Social Research. True to Gramsci's modification of Marxism-Leninism, the Frankfurt School has had a devastating impact within the walls of academia.

In one of three essays published as a short book, *A Critique of Pure Tolerance*, Marcuse authored the concluding chapter entitled, *"Repressive Tolerance."* Though the preceding text argued to re-define the notion of tolerance - possibly the cornerstone of Western Civilization - it was Marcuse who ably advanced the closing argument in an effort to solidify the idea:

> "However, this tolerance cannot be indiscriminate and equal with respect to the contents of expression, neither in word nor in deed; it cannot protect false words and wrong deeds which demonstrate they contradict and counteract the possibilities of liberation..." [source, Herbert Marcuse, A Critique of Pure Tolerance: Repressive Tolerance, p. 88]

The Orwellian nature of Marcuse's redefinition of an accepted term as a buttress to his belief system should be apparent. We also hope that the reader does not overlook the striking similarity between the left's definition of "tolerance," which is used to promote the Marxist revolutionary agenda, as being identical in practice to the Islamic concept of "defending Allah's religion" through eternal pre-emptive warfare directed against all that stands in its way.

All three of these ideas - the alternative proto-state or dual-power in Lenin's usage. socialist realism, where only that which is ideologically consistent is even granted form and substance and finally Marcuse's tortured reinvention of the touchstone upon which Western pluralistic republican democracies are based - tolerance - when combined, should demonstrate the tremendous threat that modern leftist ideology possess.

Belief systems this venomous cannot be ignored; they will never go away of their own volition. Instead, they must be actively resisted, because when lies become the standard, truth becomes the enemy.

SECULAR RELIGIONS IN FAITHLESS SOCIETIES

"Whereas other civilizations have been brought down by attacks of barbarians from without, ours had the unique distinction of training its own destroyers...and then providing them with facilities for propagating their destructive ideology far and wide...Thus did Western Man decide to abolish himself, creating his own boredom out of his own affluence, his own vulnerability out of his own strength, his own impotence out of his own erotomania, himself blowing the trumpet that brought the walls of his own city tumbling down... " - Malcolm Muggeridge

We've previously written about the seductive nature of spiritualized ideologies such as Marxism and its cultural variant in a society which has, after 170 years of profound battering, largely been denuded of traditional values

Of possible interest, this author recently published a book addressing in depth these and related issues, *Islamic Jihad Cultural Marxism and the Transformation of the West*...Amazon, at less than $15 American - check it out.

It's important to be cognizant of the process because cultural Marxism [conquest by subverting Western norms and institutions] truly represents the West's most mortal enemy. Moreover it is our belief that it's absolutely impossible [terminology which we use with great precision] to understand recent history without, at the same time, realizing that the new left is driven to extreme actions including violence by this very same sacralized belief structure.

This is the reason why you can never have a rational conversation with these people because they are in a very real sense, religious fanatics.

In what follows we have carefully selected a few passages from long-forgotten criticism by ex-Marxists, of their former ideology as a short reader of sorts. The purpose is to detail both the seductive nature of a belief system that is based on class-warfare, a triumphal sense of historical inevitability, infiltration of societies most basic institutions and a hatred of capitalism, because properly exercised it guarantees that Uncle Sam will end up binding the electorate to the state for basic sustenance in perpetuity.

The following is taken from a very disquieting book, *"The God that Failed"*, a heart-breaking testimony by those who ha become ensnared in Marx's revolutionary fairy tale

The speaker is Arthur Koestler from his chapter in the book, which is really a compilation of similar commentary that was edited by Koestler and his wife Mamaine Paget.

This is the author's remembrance of the point at which he abandoned the foundations of the West, in this particular case, logic, for the Marxist dialectical process.

"Gradually I learned to distrust my mechanistic preoccupation with facts and to regard the world around me in the light of dialectic interpretation. It was a satisfactory and indeed blissful state; once you had assimilated the technique you were no longer disturbed by facts; they automatically took on the proper color and fell into their proper place. Both morally and logically the Party was infallible: morally, because its aims were right, that is, in accord with the Dialectic of

History, and these aims justified all means; logically, because the Party was the vanguard of the Proletariat, and the Proletariat the embodiment of the active principle in History…" [Arthur Koestler, *The God that Failed*, p. 34]

Koestler here comments regarding the intellectual contortions disciples of Marx and Lenin were willing to subject themselves to in order to present the correct political face [as determined by the communist dialectic] to the enemy. Note the abrupt rejection of identifying themselves as Marxists or communists, instead embracing the term "anti-Fascist," which should provide insight into the true political ideology of the well-funded leftist street thugs who call themselves AntiFa [see, *Antifa wants combat training and firearms after losing the 'Battle for Berkeley'*, the Blaze] in that by their very choice of name they telegraph their Marxism, assuming one is conversant with the relevant history.

"The most important of these was the Seventh Congress of the Comintern in 1934, which inaugurated a new policy, a complete negation of the previous one-but to be put into effect, as always, by the same leadership. All revolutionary slogans, references to the class struggle and to the Dictatorship of the Proletariat were in one sweep relegated to the lumber room. They were replaced by a brand new facade, with geranium boxes in the windows, called "Popular Front for Peace and against Fascism." Its doors were wide open to all men of good will-Socialists, Catholics, Conservatives, Nationalists. The notion that we had ever advocated revolution and violence was to be ridiculed as a bogey refuted as a slander spread by reactionary war-mongers. We no longer referred to ourselves as "Bolsheviks," nor even as Communists-the public use of the word was now rather frowned at in the Party-we were just simple, honest, peace-loving anti-Fascists and defenders of democracy. [p. 62]

"Having experienced the almost unlimited possibilities of mental acrobatism on that tight-rope stretched across one's conscience, I know how much stretching it takes to make that elastic rope snap" [p. 72]

"Communism is the belief that society can be altered by turning men into machines for altering society." [The God that Failed, Stephen Spender, p. 271]

An unsettling parting shot is an analysis not necessarily in line with the thinking of this writer, that revolves around the changing definition of "freedom" across cultural and ethnic divisions:

"It is evident to me now that my duty is to state what I support without taking sides. Neither side, in the present alignment of the world, represents what I believe to be the only solution of the world's problems. This is: for the peoples and nations who love liberty to lead a movement throughout the world to improve the conditions of the millions of people who care more for bread than for freedom; thus raising them to a level of existence where they can care for freedom. The interests of the very few people in the world who care for the values of freedom must be identified with those of the many who need bread, or freedom will be lost." [p. 273]

So, what have we learned if anything?

Republican democracies, are - despite their numerous strengths - fragile things; like tempered glass, even under stress they can maintain tremendously strength, up to a point, past which there is no return, no rebound...atomic bonds broken ...total failure.

I am reminded of what should have been an historic speech, a particularly impassioned appeal delivered in February of 2010, at the European Parliament during the UKIP debate by British MP *Nigel Farage.*

"In generations to come, children will be told a story, that once upon a time Europe was divided, there was a big wall down the middle of it; people in the East were very poor and had no democracy. They lived under an evil system; Communism that killed millions of its own people...very sadly the politicians in charge became greedy and wanted money [and power] for themselves. They resorted to lies and deceit and staged the most spectacular bureaucratic coup d'état the world had ever seen. But they didn't need any bullets to do it. What they did was put in place a new treaty, it was called the Lisbon Treaty [giving] 27 people total unlimited power - they [built] a new state, but ignored the people and recreated the very evil system that the people in the Eastern Europe had lived under...of course the plan was flawed and collapsed *but still the new bosses wouldn't listen to the people...they made life tougher and tougher they put tens of millions into poverty, they denied the people a say and in the end those people had to resort to violence to get back their nations states and their democracy. And the moral of the story is...they had learned nothing from history.*"

Western Civilization is now engaged in a singularly distinctive, unprecedented battle for the future of the Free World. Historically, think in terms of it being the most formidable crisis we have faced in the last 500 years, predating the Reformation.

Ask yourself, am I of true heart?

Do I believe that our way of life is like a precious accident, that the West, going back to the time of Socrates, Plato and Aristotle, has been a singularly noble experiment?

Do I revere our Constitution, our democratic republic and firmly believe that man is indeed endowed by his Creator with rights that are unalienable?

If that is your creed, yet refuse to, *by any means necessary*, defeat Stalin's evil step-children, then all that we hold dear will fade into oblivion.

Quickly, the world will turn gray and shabby as if covered by industrial soot that no solvent can wash away. Brotherhood will die because men cannot be bound to each other under common purpose except upon a social contract based upon a mutual granting of liberty, freedom, tolerance and private property.

Churches, art museums, the great libraries of the world and the concert halls will empty, people pouring into the streets, milling about absent purpose - faceless, anonymous and disconsolate.

Without our beautiful things, like a body ravaged by disease the West will slowly weaken and then perish - "buried along with her name...nobody came."

We will have become, paraphrasing Orwell, smallish frail creatures, clothed in weather-beaten blue overalls...the party's uniform. Our faces? Naturally sanguine, skin rough and reddened by harsh industrial soap, dull razors, the incessant drizzle and such an overwhelming sense of hopelessness that suicide will be seen as sacramental...

And to think that all of this will have taken place, created by our own hands because so many couldn't comprehend that some things were worth fighting for...dying for. Those who have shirked their sacred responsibility will stand naked and ashamed.

Expect no pity...the judgment of our children will be cruel, unrelenting and entirely justified.

Will you remember where you were on that black morn when the sun shone not, and the last note of a Bach violin concerto quavered, in 'isochronal majesty,' off into eternity?

INDEX

Hodkinson, James, 4
Hookers, 5, 9
Hoover, FBI Director J. Edgar, 17-18
Hopkins, Harry, 35, 38-41, 45-47, 50
Hammett, Dashiell, 26-27
Horkheimer, Max, 68
Horowitz, David, 15
Johnson, President Lyndon Baines, 60, 66
Jordan, Major George "Racey", 38-47
Klehr, Harvey, 15
Koestler, Arthur, 70-71
Kotikov, Colonel Anatoli N., 44-47 49-50
Kramer, David J., 10
Lenin, Vladimir Ilych , 24-25, 33, 55, 61, 63-65, 68-69, 71
Litvinov, Soviet Commissar of Foreign Affairs Maxim, 20
Lyons, Eugene, 22
Manifesto of the Communist Party, 18
Magnitsky Act, 7
Manly, Chesly, 20, 22
Marcuse, Herbert, 68-69
Marshall, General George, 35
McCain, Senator John, 5-6
McCarthy, Senator Joseph, 27, 29, 62
McLuhan, Marshall, 4
Mission to Moscow, film, 28, 30, 46
Morgenthau, Henry Jr., 35
National Security Agency [NSA], 16
Nixon, Senator Richard M., 39, 41, 60-61
Office of War Information [OWI], 22-23, 32
Operation Barbarossa, 49
Orbis International, 7
Ossoff, John, 67
Page, Carter, 10
Poroshenko, Ukraine President Petro, 6
Putin, Russian President Vladimir, 6, 8, 10, 13, 62, 66
Reagan, President Ronald W., 14
Rhee, Jeannine, 13

,

ABOUT THE AUTHOR

William Mayer has had the pleasure of serving as the CEO/Editor & Publisher of the online national security newsletter, PipeLineNews.org LLC., for the last seventeen years. He and his wife reside in the San Francisco Bay Area

ISBN-13: 9780692939789 (PipeLineMedia)
ISBN-10: 0692939784

Made in the USA
Middletown, DE
04 August 2018